HORSE WISE GUIDES

W9-BZO-683

Getting Your
First Horse

Judith Dutson

Foreword by John Lyons

Storey Publishing

The mission of Storey Publishing is to serve our customers
by publishing practical information that encourages personal independence
in harmony with the environment.

Edited by Elizabeth McHale and Marie Salter
Cover design by Meredith Maker
Cover photograph © Gemma Giannini
Text design by Faith Hague and Susan Bernier
Text production by Susan Bernier
Photographs by Lisa Helfert, except where noted
Illustrations by James E. Dyekman
Indexed by Susan Olason/Indexes & Knowledge Maps

The information in this book is true and complete to the best of our knowledge. All recommendations are made without guarantee on the part of the author or Storey Publishing. The author and publisher disclaim any liability in connection with the use of this information. For additional information, please contact Storey Publishing, 210 MASS MoCA Way, North Adams, MA 01247.

Storey books are available for special premium and promotional uses and for customized editions. For further information, please call 800-793-9396.

Printed in Canada by Transcontinental Printing
10 9 8 7

Library of Congress Cataloging-in-Publication Data

Dutson, Judith.
    Getting your first horse / Judith Dutson.
        p.   cm. — (Horse-wise guides series)
    Includes bibliographical references (p.) and index.
    ISBN 1-58017-078-1
    1. Horses. 2. Horsemanship. I. Title. II. Series: Horse-wise guides.
    IN PROCESS
        636.1'081—dc21   98-25941
                                                                                                    CIP

DEDICATION

To Do Go Jo,
who at thirty-two has been a
special friend for twenty-six years,
and to Dodo, and Apples, and Scout,
and all the horses in between
who taught me what to do.

Contents

Foreword

Judith Dutson has done both the prospective horse owner and the first-time horse buyer a tremendous service in writing this book. The information provided here will save horse owners a great deal of time, money, and heartache, because it provides them with the knowledge they need to buy and care for a horse responsibly.

Because of this book, undoubtedly many horses will live in safer environments, receive better care, and live longer, simply because their owners will know how to improve and properly maintain the worlds in which horses live.

Looking for a horse can be confusing. There are so many variables to consider that it's easy to become overwhelmed. *Getting Your First Horse* guides you through the process, offering helpful information on size, color, breed, age, and conformation, as well as on how to determine the level of experience you'd like in a horse. Perhaps most importantly, this book helps you assess your own needs, which, when coupled with your personal riding goals, will lead you to the best horse for you.

To many people, horses are simply beautiful creatures. But prospective horse owners and riders should look beyond appearances and know that there are many differences between individual horses and that sometimes those differences can get you hurt. Temperament, soundness, and vices are discussed in detail to educate you to all the possibilities, good and bad.

Some would have us believe that the more you pay, the more you get. That's not necessarily so in many situations in life and particularly not when purchasing a horse. Quite often a prospective buyer may pay more because of some sentimental attachment an owner has for a horse. Buyers can also spend far more than they should if they don't know how to thoroughly evaulate a horse's temperament, conformation, and potential. For horse and owner to be happy, it's important that the horse be healthy, sound, and capable of doing what the owner expects. The section on veterinary prepurchase exams is essential reading, particularly if you're not sure how to evaluate a horse and don't know how good a horse's conformation must be to suit your riding needs.

Judith Dutson is exceedingly careful when discussing many of the mistakes first-time owners make. Though many of us have learned these lessons the hard way, with this book others are sure to fare much better. The educated horse owner is the best horse owner, and this book goes a long way to educating all of us.

Getting Your First Horse has much to offer first-time horse buyers and horse owners in general. Every barn and professional trainer should keep several copies on hand to loan to people who are thinking about buying their first horse or another horse. I recommend this book because it is full of valuable information on how to buy, care for, and enjoy our equine friends.

— John Lyons

ACKNOWLEDGMENTS

I thank the following people for their encouragement and help in the production of this book: Jane O'Reilly, Katherine Bradford, Jody Hoch, Anne Bartley, Steve Schumacher, Carol Crowl, Cindy Bowers, Lori Kipp, John Lyons, Dale Evans, Elizabeth McHale, Marie Salter, and Kevin Kearney.

Before You Buy

You've waited all your life to have a horse, and now you think it's time to get one. You're probably thinking about the kind of horse you want, what color you'd like him to be, and maybe even what to name him. A better place to start, though, is by thinking about yourself or your child — whoever will be the principal rider in the family. Think, too, about how much you know about horses, how much time you have to put into caring for a horse, and how you want to develop your riding skills. This will provide important information that will help guide you as you begin to shop for a horse and make decisions about how you're going to care for him. *Then* it's time to start thinking about the horse!

The Rider

Your goals with your first horse should be to have a good time, learn more, and learn to ride better. The better this horse is suited to you, the more likely you are to enjoy yourself, horse ownership, and the sport of riding.

We're all inclined to overestimate our knowledge of horses, but try to be honest with yourself regarding just how much you really know. Do you have a good foundation in the basics of riding? For the sake of safety, it's wise to consider anyone who has ridden seriously for less than three years as a beginner. Some people who have ridden many more years than this are still beginners because they haven't had the time or desire to go beyond the basics, while others haven't had the benefit of good instruction.

Riding Lessons

Do plan on taking lessons with your first horse from a competent instructor. The instructor can help you learn the ways of your horse, while the horse learns about you. Your instructor can also ensure that neither of you develops any bad habits.

▲
Choose a horse that's well behaved, patient, and even tempered.

Here are some questions to consider when assessing your knowledge:

✓ Have you only had riding lessons?
✓ Do you understand the fundamentals of horsemanship?
✓ Have you developed any finesse as a rider?
✓ Can you put on a halter, or saddle and bridle a horse yourself?
✓ Do you know how to groom a horse?
✓ Do you know basic safety rules for working with horses?

The answer to these questions should play an important role in selecting your horse.

The less experience you have, the more important it is to buy a horse that's well behaved, patient, and even tempered.

Starting Out Safely

When selecting your first horse, there is one absolute rule that you should consider sacred. Don't break it under any circumstances, no matter how tempting: *Inexperienced riders must not work with inexperienced horses.*

The *Black Stallion* books were great stories and the basis for beautiful movies, but they don't represent the real world. Each time you handle a horse, you teach the horse something; good or bad, the horse is always learning from you. Generally, beginners don't realize what or how much the horse learns from them: They don't know how to respond appropriately and quickly, and they don't know how best to teach the horse what it is they want to convey. Likewise, an inexperienced horse doesn't understand the rider's expectations. For these reasons and for your own safety, if you are inexperienced, you should *not* work with an inexperienced horse.

Temperament

Although the horse's disposition is an important consideration that you'll read more about later, consider your own temperament, too. If you're the kind of person who flies off the handle quickly, there are some individual horses, and maybe some breeds, that would be better for you than others.

If you tend to be the short-tempered or impatient type, it would be a good idea to get a quiet, even-tempered, experienced horse. Then work on thinking before you react, because even the most docile horse can and will spook if provoked. Anger is the most difficult emotion for many people to control, but it's also incompatible with good horse handling. To quote the famous horseman John Lyons: "Anger is the wind that blows out the candle of the mind." You need to keep that candle lit. Never lose your temper with a horse.

If the rider will be a child, the issues of temper and temperament may be even more important than they are for adults. For a child with a short fuse, the horse must have an exceptionally even disposition, and the child should be supervised at all times when with the horse, whether that's on the ground or in the saddle. All horses can be frustrating now and then. With proper guidance, however, the quick-tempered, easily frustrated child can learn to remain calm to help the horse give his best performance.

Similarly, a quiet, well-trained, steady horse will help bring out the best in a timid rider.

Time

You may want to ride every day, but consider whether that's a realistic notion. The time you have available is an important consideration before you buy a horse, because horses need regular attention. At some boarding stables, the boarders are expelled if they don't appear at the barn at least three times a week!

It's also unfair to a horse to keep him in a stall most days of the week, then ride him hard on weekends. If you really want to own a horse, you'll have to make time for him, even in cold, unpleasant weather. Three rides a week is a reasonable average for adults with jobs. Children usually want to ride more. Some young riders will need to be pried off the horse to preserve the animal's health and happiness!

Budget

Of course, there's the matter of paying for your horse. It takes some money to properly care for one. In addition, a horse can end up costing more than you ever thought possible if you don't do your homework. Your initial purchase price could be anywhere from $500 to more than $5,000. But it's the upkeep you really need to consider, which includes the cost of boarding your horse or of keeping him at home, equipment, and supplies. Check out chapter 5 to get a better handle on everything you'll need, but before you begin shopping, just remember that money is an important consideration.

Options for the Physically Challenged

If you or your child has physical limitations, a horse can still be a part of your life, and he may be helpful as well as being fun. A number of riding programs throughout the United States feature instructors trained to work with the physically challenged and those with emotional problems. Riding in these programs has been shown to improve muscle strength and coordination for children with diseases such as cerebral palsy. It also improves self-esteem.

If you're a disabled adult or have a disabled child who's unable to ride, driving horses may be an option. Carts can be adapted to accommodate wheelchairs fairly easily. If full-size horses are too intimidating, well-selected miniature driving animals may be your answer.

Of course, you should always investigate a riding program carefully to make sure it provides well-trained instructors and safe horses. With a little bit of pluck and perseverance, though, you'll find many more opportunities with horses for the physically challenged than you thought possible.

Riding Goals

In order to choose the best horse for the job, you need to have some idea of what the horse's job will be. This will be dictated by your riding plans and goals.

Arena Work

If you don't have access to miles of trails or don't like trail riding, but you do like the intellectual as well as physical exercise of improving your riding, you may plan to work primarily in an arena. Many exercises developed for both English and Western riders can be done in an arena, and will improve your harmony with your horse as well as advance your riding skills. Make sure you vary your routine often so the horse has as much fun as you do. (See Recommended Reading for more on arena exercises.)

Trail Riding

You may want to enjoy the trails and have noncompetitive fun with your horse. If this is your primary interest, you don't need a fancy horse suited to the show ring. Instead, you might consider breeds with special

▶
There are many exercises you can do in an arena that will improve your harmony with your horse as well as advance your riding skills.

gaits, such as Tennessee Walkers, Paso Finos, or Rocky Mountain Horses. These horses aren't ideal for learning to jump, but they can provide a very comfortable ride and often make great trail animals.

If you like trail riding but may want to compete one day, too, there are competitive trail rides and endurance rides. The horses best suited to this kind of work are usually midsize or smaller, and not heavily muscled. Arabian geldings are widely used, because they can develop tremendous endurance with proper conditioning. Very bulky horses, such as the heavily muscled, old-style Quarter Horses, don't, as a rule, fare quite as well, even with a good conditioning program.

Show Riding

If you're interested in competing, there are horse shows for almost every breed of horse, every type of riding, and every level of riding. Go to some of these shows to see what interests you most. You may want to learn to jump or to tackle the discipline of dressage. Or maybe you prefer the speed of contest events, the grace of saddleseat riding, or the fun of driving a horse. Whatever you select, there's sure to be a show for you somewhere. (See Recommended Reading for some books on various horse show topics.)

The most popular horse show class in the country is Western Pleasure. In a Western Pleasure class, riders are asked to walk, jog, and lope in both directions around the arena. It sounds easy, but because the classes are so popular, the judges have many entrants to choose from and the competition can be stiff.

Other popular Western events are reining, in which each horse and rider work a predetermined pattern individually; and cutting, in which you and your horse demonstrate your ability to cut, or separate, one steer from a herd and prevent it from rejoining the herd until you choose to allow it.

◄
In a Western Pleasure class, riders are asked to walk, jog, and lope around the arena. (AQHA photo by Wyatt McSpadden.)

Cutting and reining require skills that take years to master. Timed Western contest events, such as barrel racing and pole bending, are also popular.

Those who favor English riding sports have a wide assortment of activities to select from. One type of English riding, called saddleseat riding, is seen at American Saddlebred Horse, Morgan, Arabian, and Tennessee Walking Horse shows, as well as a few others.

▶

Saddleseat riding is just one of many English-style riding sports. (Photo by Jamie Donaldson; courtesy of The American Saddlebred Horse Association, Inc.)

Another type of English riding is jumping. You'll see this at hunter/jumper shows, as well as in classes at Quarter Horse, Morgan, and Appaloosa shows. Many people are confused by the terms *hunter* and *jumper.* In the jumper division, the horses are scored by how many jumping faults — knocking down rails and refusing fences — they accumulate in a round. The rounds are also scored for time. If there are two or more horses with no jumping faults, they come back and jump higher fences, trying to do so in the shortest possible time. In this division it doesn't matter how pretty the horse looks going over a jump; it just matters that he get to the other side without knocking something down.

In the hunter division, however, the horses are judged on how perfectly they jump each fence. Form counts. The judges score horses based on how they meet and jump each obstacle, as well as on each one's manners and "way of going." (*Way of going* is the total picture — soundness, correctness of movement, impulsion, and carriage. Is he tugging on the reins or does he have to be pushed? Does he look interested in his work or bored?)

Riders who like to jump may enjoy showing in the hunter division at shows or may prefer to join a local hunt and go fox hunting — a sport that's alive and flourishing in many parts of the United States. Some hunts in this country are live hunts, but in locations where foxes are rare, foxes are chased rather than killed. Only foxes that are injured or obviously diseased are killed in these areas. One such hunt in Ohio has killed only three foxes since 1968. Drag hunts that follow an artificial scent train and never kill anything are another option.

A third type of English riding is dressage. Riders who enjoy competing in dressage usually do so at dressage shows, which are open to any breed of horse, or at those breed shows that have a dressage division. At its highest level, dressage is the most formal and elegant of the Olympic equestrian events, but dressage shows also have many classes for less experienced horses and riders. In fact, it's expected that horses and riders will progress through a series of classes as they develop skill.

▲
Fox hunting is alive and flourishing in many parts of the United States. (Photo courtesy of Masters of Foxhounds Association of America.)

Combined Training/Eventing

Eventing encompasses three different disciplines of riding. It grew out of military exercises designed to test the skills and bravery of cavalry officers and their horses. The first discipline is dressage, mentioned above, which is really a test of willingness, obedience, and precision: The horses individually perform a series of prescribed movements and are judged on their skill at each movement. The second discipline is cross-country riding, in which the horses jump a series of more or less natural-looking obstacles that may include creeks, fences, and ditches. The third discipline, stadium jumping, involves jumping a course of fences inside a show ring. Eventing is not just a sport for Olympic athletes; there are many levels, starting with tests for novice horses and riders.

Driving

For those who like horse sports but don't want to ride, consider driving horses. Some people drive around their farms or down quiet lanes, but you can also show anything from spitfire Hackneys to elegant Saddlebred or Morgan park harness horses and single or multiple hitches of Haflingers. If big horses are intimidating, miniature horses make good driving animals.

The growing sport of combined driving involves dressage, obstacle, and cross-country driving. If you like speed, there are roadster divisions at Hackney, Morgan, Shetland, and Saddlebred shows. Want to go even faster? Work toward a license to drive Standardbred harness racers.

▲
Dressage shows in which riders of all levels can compete are held throughout the United States. (Photo by Terri Miller; courtesy of the American Hanoverian Horse Society.)

Other Riding Options

There are hundreds of horse sports, from jousting to riding in parades. There are equestrian drill teams and mounted search-and-rescue riders. There are trick and fancy riding groups and calf-roping clubs. There are Civil War reenactment riding troupes and polo teams, ladies' sidesaddle-riding clubs, team penning groups, and Shriners-mounted patrols. You don't have to commit yourself to any sport yet, but it will be easier to find the right sort of horse if you have a good idea what type of riding you intend to pursue.

The Horse

Once you've thought about yourself, your strengths and shortcomings regarding horses, and your budget, it's time to start thinking about the horse. I'll go into more detail in the next chapter, but following are some of the general characteristics you'll want to think about before you begin shopping. They'll help provide direction as you search for your first horse.

Size

You've probably attended horse shows in which all the riders seemed to be mounted on gigantic, bold, beautiful steeds. You may find as you talk to people about horses and look at ads in the paper that there seems to be a great deal of interest in horses that are 16 hands (16h) tall or larger.

Very large horses do make a beautiful picture, but you'll have a much better time if your horse is a more appropriate size for you. An average-size riding horse is probably about 14.3h to 15.3h tall, and this is a reasonable size unless you're very tall, heavy, or tiny. In addition, a horse 16h or larger may cost substantially more than a similar horse that's just a little bit smaller. You may well save yourself some money by looking at the slightly smaller fellows. Of course, size is not your only consideration, nor is it the most important one; it's just a convenient place to start as you begin thinking about the horse you want.

A moderate-size horse is also practical. He'll be easier to get up onto, especially for the short or short legged. Furthermore, when you ride, you influence the horse with your leg, urging him with your heels to go forward and also giving other subtle instructions. If you're short or short legged, you may not be able to use your legs effectively on a big horse, especially while you're learning to ride. You'll do better with a horse of more average size. On the other hand, if you're built like a professional basketball player, you won't want a pony you can lock your feet around.

If you're a heavy person, a good-size horse with a sturdy conformation is in order, but don't assume you need a horse that's tall. A stocky horse of 15.3h may be better able to carry your weight than a slender horse of 17h, because the taller animal has a higher center of gravity and may not be able to balance as well as the stockier one.

Although correct riding doesn't require great strength, strength can be an issue. People with weak arms or bad necks, or children who are small for their age or younger than about 12 years old may find it hard to handle a large, strong horse, even if he's got a calm temperament. It's kind of like driving a big car: A small person can handle a big car if it has power steering; if there's no power steering, however, a small car would be easier to drive. Likewise, if the horse feels difficult to "steer" and stop, keep looking for one that suits you.

If you're buying a horse for a child about to hit a growth spurt, avoid getting a pony that the child will quickly outgrow. Try instead to find a horse that will remain somewhere in the reasonable size range for a couple of years yet to come.

▲
Try to find a horse that's a size suitable for you. This rider and horse are well matched.

Horse Height

Horses are measured in units called hands. Each hand is 4 inches. The horse is measured in a straight line from the ground to the highest point of his withers. A mature animal larger than 14 hands 2 inches (14.2h) is a true horse. A mature animal that's less than 14.2h is a pony. If the animal is exactly 14.2h, you may consider it either a true horse or a pony, but if you show you must pick one division and stick with it.

Gender

Geldings are castrated male horses. Most horsemen find them to have the most even dispositions. Of course, there are geldings that don't have great dispositions, but usually a well-chosen gelding is a steady sort of fellow.

Mares are female horses. Some people think all mares are witchy because of their heat cycles and hormonal influences. Some mares become nervous or maybe a little nasty for a few days each month. They might be hard to ride, unpleasant to other horses, or — in the worst cases — unpleasant to people. Some mares seem just mildly distracted, and many show no behavioral changes at all.

The truth is that some mares are periodically witchy and some aren't. If you find a mare that has a nice disposition, and you like everything else about her, don't take her off your list of candidates just because she's a mare. Do be aware that some days with her might be better than others. If you find yourself with a mare that has bigger mood swings due to estrus than you anticipated, there are effective drugs that can be administered to help, but they may be expensive.

What you want to avoid for your first horse is a stallion, a male horse capable of breeding. Some stallions are well-behaved fellows, but they're always harder to handle than geldings because they have the potential to become dangerous without warning. Stallions are never appropriate for a beginning rider, a new horse owner, or a child.

Color

The color of your horse isn't nearly as important as his temperament, health (see chapter 2), and suitability for your needs. Most of us, however, do consider the color of a horse when we're buying one. Some colors appeal to us and some don't. It's nice to have a horse you think is attractive; just don't make color your main consideration.

You'll want to learn about horse colors so you'll have an idea what the horse looks like as you talk to people or perhaps read ads. Here are some of the basic horse colors:

Black: This is a completely black animal with an entirely black muzzle and no lighter color on the inside of the legs above the knees. Many horses that look black in winter will shed out to brown on muzzle or legs; these are called dark-brown horses.

Brown: This horse has a brown muzzle and a dark brown to black coat.

Bay: A red, reddish, or brown coat with black points. (*Points* are the mane, tail, lower legs, and tips of the ears.)

Chestnut: Chestnuts are red horses; the mane is the same color as the body of the horse. Chestnut is a term recognized by the Jockey Club and the Morgan, Arabian, Saddlebred, and Standardbred Associations, as well as some others. These groups never use the word *sorrel* to designate a red coat.

Sorrel: Sorrel means red. This word is associated with Quarter Horses, Appaloosas, Paints, and a few others. The associations and registries for these breeds never use the word *chestnut* to mean red.

Palomino: The coat is a gold to yellow color and the mane and tail are cream, silvery, or white.

Buckskin: A dull, light brown shade accompanied by a darker stripe down the back, called a dorsal stripe.

Gray: A gray coat or a white coat, sometimes with dapples. A gray horse has a dark coat when he's born that lightens with age. He's different from a white horse, because he has dark skin.

White: A white horse was born white and has pink skin and a pink muzzle. Like the black horse, a truly white horse is unusual.

Roan: Roans have a basic body color, such as sorrel, and some individual hairs that are two colors: the basic body color and white. A roan's color is a muted version of the basic body color. If it is a chestnut or sorrel horse, it is called a *red roan*. If the body color is black or dark brown, the horse will appear to be blue-gray and so is called a *blue roan*. Bay roans are rare but quite beautiful.

There are advantages and disadvantages to each of the various coat colors, but they're relatively minor. Just so you know, however: White, light gray, palomino, and pinto can be harder to keep looking spiffy. They show dirt more easily than other colors, and the horses seem to seek out dirt.

Horses with a great deal of white also can sunburn easily, although there are sunscreens available to help you cope if this becomes a problem. Ranchers who ride horses long and hard dislike white in the girth area, because it seems to get saddle sores more easily than do darker hides. Some — but not all — white hooves crack, chip, and break more easily than dark ones. But in today's world of pleasure riding and given the common use of horseshoes, you probably needn't worry much about hoof problems associated with lack of color.

White Markings

Many people like the look of a horse with some white markings. If someone tells you a horse has a white blaze, that means white comes down his face from forehead to muzzle. If most of the horse's face is white, that's known as a bald face. White just on the forehead is known as a star, and a narrow patch of white down the face is called a strip. A horse can have a star and strip. A snip is a small bit of white between the nostrils.

Many horses have white markings on their legs. Socks are white markings that extend from the hoof to just above the fetlock. If white extends from the hoof farther up the leg, it's called a stocking.

> ### Points
>
> Points on a horse refer to the tips of his ears, legs, mane, and tail. Horses that are bays have black points: Their manes, tails, and ear tips are black, as is the lower part of their legs.

Horse Age

Good veterinary care and worming programs are allowing horses to live much longer than they used to. Most horses live into their 20s, many into their 30s. Some ponies live to be 40.

You probably don't want to purchase an antique, which might be thought of as a horse in his mid-20s or older. He may have the aches and pains of old age, and he might develop problems that would prevent you from riding him as much as you'd like to, or maybe even from riding at all. You shouldn't buy an old horse that you might have to retire in a few years. Old horses are harder to sell than younger ones. For some riders, however, this isn't a problem. They keep but retire their old horse, and buy another younger animal to ride. Whether you can do this will depend on your ability to support two horses. Before you buy an old horse, think about what you'll do with him if he has to be retired.

If you buy a "teenaged" horse and keep him until he's in his 20s, you might have a problem when you try to sell him, but a sound horse in his teens or even early 20s could give you many years of riding pleasure, especially if he's ridden reasonably. Older horses are very often great teachers because they have the wisdom of experience. For example, old dressage horses that can no longer compete are often sold for high prices as "schoolmasters." These horses can be used to teach riders how to use subtle cues. If the rider gets it wrong, the horse won't perform the movement.

An older horse that's in good shape will stay in good health longest if kept in work. Don't exhaust the horse, but keep him at a constant level of fitness. An old horse that gets very soft and out of shape will have to be brought back into work slowly and carefully.

A wise first buyer will probably steer clear of a horse four years of age or younger. Five years might be a better lower age limit, all other things being equal. Of course, all other things never will be equal, so age is just one of many factors to consider. But do keep in mind that important safety rule: Inexperienced riders must never ride inexperienced horses. Generally, this makes a young horse a poor choice, even if he seems calm.

Horse Birthdays

All horses have the same official birthday, which is January 1 of the year they were born. From the time a foal is born until he's weaned, he's known as a suckling. Once he's separated from his mother, he's known as a weanling. On January 1 of the next year, the foal officially becomes a yearling. On the following January 1, he becomes a two-year-old.

If the foal is male, he's a colt until he turns four years old, at which time he becomes a horse. A male horse that's been castrated is called a gelding. A male horse that is not castrated is a stallion. If the foal is female, she's known as a filly until she turns four years old, at which time she becomes a mare.

Temperament

Buy a horse that you can handle and enjoy right from the start. Avoid a horse with behavior or training problems. If you have to enlist the help of a trainer, it's expensive, and unless you select the trainer very carefully you could end up with a big training bill and a horse that still has problems.

A horse you can handle is going to be one with an even temperament and good manners. He's calm and obedient; he stands nicely while you mount or dismount, moves off when you give him the aids to walk, trot, or canter, and has good "brakes" — he stops readily when you ask. A calm, well-behaved horse isn't fidgety and doesn't frighten easily. He's obedient whether other horses are around or not. He doesn't bolt, buck, or rear. (Rearing, by the way, is considered an especially dangerous behavior, because a horse that rears can fall over backward and on top of you.)

Ground manners also indicate temperament. If a horse bites with intent to do harm, leave him for somebody else. If a horse kicks when the girth is fastened, or consistently turns his tail toward you when you enter the stall, you don't want him.

Reading Body Language

To judge a horse's temperament, you need to know something about horse body language. Putting the ears forward toward you in a relaxed manner as you approach indicates the horse is interested and acting in a friendly manner.

The horse that pins his ears back against his head for no apparent reason when you approach, or that also bares his teeth, is acting in a threatening manner. Swishing the tail is another sign of aggression or unease. A horse that turns his hind end toward you when you approach the stall door may or may not be aggressive, but he's certainly being uncooperative. This behavior is dangerous. In such a case, do not enter the stall; the horse must face you before you enter.

Horse Background

What a horse has done in the past can provide clues about how he'll respond in the future. Former barrel-racing or contest horses and ex-racehorses may not be the best choice for new riders and horse owners, because they've been trained to move out fast. Ponies that have previously been owned by children who loved to go fast can be equally poor choices. Your goal is to find a quiet horse that enjoys going for a ride with you.

In contrast, a horse that was another beginning rider's pleasure horse, or perhaps one used in a school program for beginning riders (as long as he is not sour about beginning riders), is far more likely to be a horse you can handle and one that you'll enjoy — and that's what you want!

2

What to Look for in a Horse

AS YOU SEARCH FOR A HORSE, you'll soon come to realize that horses are as individual as people, and that none is perfect. Horses are beautiful animals, but as wise horsemen know, pretty is as pretty does. Sometimes, beautiful horses may not work out. Some seemingly small faults in conformation can cause big problems. And some plain horses or horses considered less than beautiful by human standards can be wonderful pleasure mounts or fantastic athletes because they're well built. In this chapter, you'll learn to spot imperfections and decide which ones you can live with and which you can't.

Conformation

Conformation means the way the horse is put together, or conformed. Her function follows her form. How the horse is put together will determine how comfortably and efficiently she'll be able to move and carry you.

Horse conformation has been studied seriously for as long as horses have been kept by humans. In past generations, horses were a major means of transportation for people and were essential for military transport. Horses that were comfortable to ride and held up to hard work were as important then as tanks, jeeps, and airplanes are today. In virtually every society in the world that rode, therefore, the military put a great deal of effort into studying what made a good, useful horse. They pretty much all came to similar conclusions about desirable basic structures, which are the guidelines of horse conformation common to all breeds.

Many books are written about horse conformation. Read as many as you can, and familiarize yourself with the good and bad points of horses. Be aware that conformation books and articles tend to emphasize the ideal; in the real world, nothing is quite perfect. If you want to learn even more about conformation, observe many horses; it's a good way to get a handle on different conformation traits and will help you decide what you like and what you don't. (See Recommended Readings for suggested videos.)

Head

Most people look at a horse's head first and many select or reject the animal based on her head, but this can be a mistake: The head doesn't make the horse. Someone who falls in love with a pretty-headed horse may easily overlook the bad legs that could make her inappropriate for riding. A plain-headed horse might be very useful, and you might get her even cheaper because of her appearance. Learn to evaluate the whole horse, not just the head. Remember, pretty is as pretty does.

Head shapes are usually a matter of taste and fashion. Arabians are selected to have the dished profile characteristic of the breed. In Standard-breds and Hackneys, there's much less preference for any particular head shape, and you'll find some individuals with Roman noses. In Quarter Horses, the profile is usually flat but some emphasis is placed on the head being short from eye to nostril. Ancient Greeks didn't favor horses that were short from the eye to the nostril; they thought it made the animals look like cows.

A dished profile is characteristic of the Arabian.

In Quarter Horses, the profile is generally shorter from eye to muzzle than in other horses, such as the Thoroughbred.

This horse has a Roman nose.

Eyes

The eyes are important. You'll certainly want to avoid a horse with impaired vision, because she may not be safe to ride. Before you buy a horse, the eyes should be examined by a veterinarian, who has special equipment that can help detect problems that may cause blindness or distorted vision. More on the prepurchase veterinary examination appears later in this chapter (see page 34).

The relative size of the eyes is a factor to be taken into account. Small-eyed horses are referred to as pig eyed, and many horsemen are wary of them. They believe these animals tend to be skittish or even downright bad tempered, and there may be some truth to this piece of lore.

To understand why, you need to know something about how most horses see. They can see straight in front of their faces, but because their eyes are situated toward the sides of their heads, they don't have binocular vision up close to their faces. They also see well to the side, and can even see something behind them by bending their necks just a bit. They're particularly well designed to see movement, including even a tiny movement a fair distance away. All of this allows the horse to see danger in plenty of time to get out of the way, a crucial adaptation in a prey species.

A pig-eyed horse may not have the extent of peripheral vision that other horses do, so a moving object coming from the rear or the side might surprise her. In self-defense, the horse spooks. People may think that the horse is behaving badly and react by punishing her inappropriately, which

▲

Many horsemen consider horses with larger eyes, such as this one, to be preferable to those with small eyes. (Photo by Ann Bartley.)

▲

Small-eyed horses are referred to as "pig eyed."

could make her behavior worse. Small eyes alone aren't a reason to eliminate a horse from your list of candidates if you like everything else about her; just be aware of the pig-eyed horse's problem. You'll need to handle her reasonably and always strive to maintain her confidence.

Mouth

Mouth conformation is important because the bit has to fit well and comfortably if you're to communicate lightly and effectively with your horse.

The most common jaw deformity is called parrot mouth, and it's equivalent to an overbite in people. In most cases, a parrot mouth is minor and not too much to worry about, especially if you're a pleasure rider who doesn't want to show. Parrot mouth may be unsightly, but usually causes no real harm.

In severe cases, however, the lower jaw is malformed and the horse can't wear a bit. Some severely parrot-mouthed horses may even have trouble eating grass and maintaining their weight. Or they may swallow big lumps of poorly chewed food and make themselves sick.

Parrot mouth is considered to be a serious fault, and it's heritable, so you shouldn't consider breeding an animal with it. The condition will be a problem if you want to show your horse in a conformation class, because judges will hold it as a serious fault against her. More than the plain-headed horse, the seriously parrot-mouthed horse will be hard to sell, even

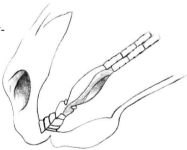

▲

This horse has a parrot mouth.

if she's wonderful in every other way. Mildly parrot-mouthed horses, especially geldings, are usually saleable. If you'll need to sell her when you become a more advanced rider, consider this problem before you buy.

A far less common problem, but one you may want to be aware of, is an injured tongue from the use of severe bits or other training devices. Such horses may not be able to wear a bit and some may not be able to eat normally, which could lead to chronic colic problems. To be sure that any horse you want to buy can wear a bit and eat comfortably, check the tongue when you look at the horse, or make sure the veterinarian does in the prepurchase exam.

Withers

The withers can be easily identified: They're the part of the horse where the neck meets the back. Most horses have a little hump there. It might be compared with the nape of your neck.

In some horses, especially Thoroughbreds, the withers are very high. It's important to make sure that the saddle you use doesn't pinch the withers. A saddler can help you determine if a saddle fits correctly. If you have a saddle that doesn't fit your horse, you need to get one that does, because pinched withers can really hurt her.

At the other end of the scale are horses with very low withers, called "mutton-withered" horses. This fault is more difficult to live with, because the withers are what help keep the saddle in place. With a mutton-withered horse, the saddle will shift, which is annoying to you and can chafe and annoy your horse as well. You can live with slightly low withers, but if the horse is really mutton withered, riding long distances up and down hills might present a problem.

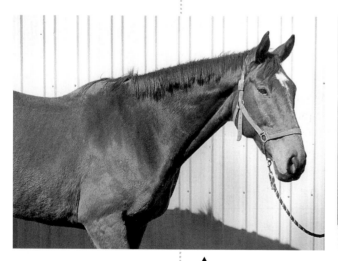 

▲
The horse on the left has high withers; the horse on the right, low withers.

Feet and Legs

The legs and feet have the potential for causing more problems than anything else on a horse. Educate yourself to the best of your ability on conformation of the legs and feet.

Feet

Look for a horse with feet large enough to support the animal. Having some idea of the relative size of feet that are appropriate for a given horse is something that can only be learned by looking at many horses, so start training your eye now.

Small feet on a large horse is potentially a serious problem, because it predisposes the animal to various forms of lameness. Unfortunately, there are conformation show judges who like to see horses with small, "tidy" feet. As a consequence, some horses intended to be shown in Halter classes are being bred to have tiny feet. They look pretty in the show ring as youngsters, but they don't hold up well as they mature and gain weight. This is especially a problem in Quarter Horses, Paints, and Appaloosas that have been bred for the halter ring. It doesn't mean you should avoid these breeds, but do watch out for inappropriately small feet in them.

Also beware of horses with foot conformation that's been "corrected" to appear normal. The problem arises when less-than-ideal feet are artfully shaped and trimmed to make them look ideal; such feet and legs may no longer effectively absorb concussion. The end result could be a horse that looks great but has chronically sore feet and is, or will be, lame.

It will take a good veterinarian or farrier to identify a horse that's been trimmed in this way. It's something you're more likely to find in horses shown in the conformation ring, so if a seller brags about a horse's halter wins, be cautious. A horse with less attractive feet may not be as pretty, but she *may* stay sound much longer, depending on the problems. Discuss it with your veterinarian.

Legs

Straight legs are something all conformation books talk about at great length. If you're standing in front of the horse and drop a plumb line from the point of her shoulder to the ground, it should bisect her leg; run through the middle of her knee, down the middle of her cannon bone, through the middle of her ankle, and, finally, through the middle of her hoof.

Straight legs are important because the legs receive a great deal of concussive force every time the horse takes a step. The faster she's traveling, the more force each leg receives. If her legs are straight, then they can work the way they were meant to, as shock absorbers. If the horse has crooked legs, however, the forces of concussion will be directed out of line, and some body part that isn't really built to absorb the full brunt of it will get it. This may well cause problems for your horse and thus for you.

The Four-S Test

There's a lot to remember as you look at horses. If you need help, though, just remember the four Ss:

✓ Sound
✓ Sane
✓ Safe
✓ Suitable

Any horse you buy should be all of these things.

Front Legs

Most books on conformation go to quite some length to tell you about horses that are base narrow, which means wide at the chest and narrow at the feet. Base-wide horses are narrow at the chest and wide at the feet. You'll also learn about horses that toe in, which means they're pigeon toed, and horses that toe out, which is, of course, just the opposite.

Offset knees is a serious fault in racehorses. If you look at such a horse from the front, you'll see that the long bone that comes from the shoulder down to the knee doesn't appear to meet with the long bone running from knee to ankle. Sometimes the long axis of one or both knees almost looks diagonal instead of vertical. In racehorses, this fault almost guarantees serious knee problems, but in a horse whose speed is not a big issue, it's not so worrisome. This is another fault that seems to be heritable, so you don't want to select a horse with offset knees if you plan to breed down the road.

Horses legs also are judged from the side. Some have a condition known as being "over at the knee." In pronounced cases, the knees look like they're about to buckle and the horse to fall down, although she won't.

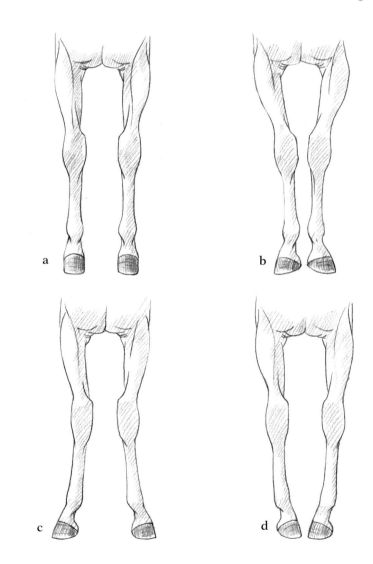

▶

Foreleg conformation, front view: good legs (a), base narrow (b), base wide (c), toed in (d).

Horses that are over at the knee generally look worse than the problem will be for you to live with. In fact, many old show and field hunters have this condition, but are still able to go out and do their jobs.

Horses back at the knee are just the opposite: The front of the knee looks flat, but the back of the leg behind the knee looks hyperextended. This is a serious fault in a racehorse, a jumper, or a contest horse, but probably won't cause much harm in a pleasure horse. Again, though, stay away from these problems if you ever plan to breed.

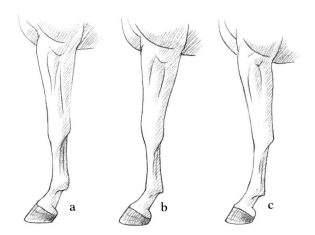

▲

Foreleg conformation, side view: good legs (a), over at knee (b), back at knee (c).

Hind Legs

The hind legs have their own set of possible faults. As seen from the side, the horse can be sickle hocked, which means that her hocks are not of ideal shape. In a normal stance, a sickle-hocked horse will carry her hind legs too far under her body.

Although sickle hocks are less-than-perfect conformation for most horses, some horsemen prefer a mild case of it in animals to be used for reining and cutting (because they have to nearly sit down in their athletic work) and in show Tennessee Walkers (which must take huge steps with their back legs). The opposite fault is seen in horses that structurally carry their hind legs too far out behind.

As seen from the rear, the horse can be base wide or base narrow; she can also be cow hocked, which is comparable to having knock knees at the back end. For most horses, cow hocks are less than perfect, but in draft horses that pull huge loads cow hocks are desirable. Again, some riders of reining or cutting horses don't mind a horse that's a little bit cow hocked.

Horses that look bow legged when seem from the tail end view are said to be bandy legged. In any but the least-active riding horses, this conformation fault is likely to cause serious hock problems.

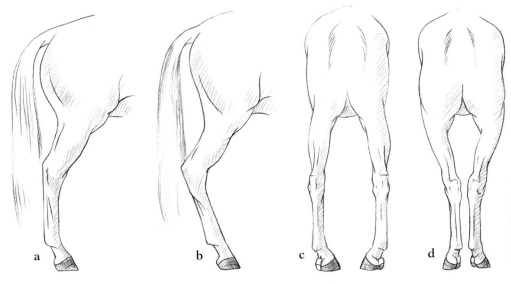

◀

Hind leg conformation, side view: good (a), sickle hocked (b); rear view: bandy legged (c), cow hocked (d).

Pasterns

The pasterns are the sections of lower leg that extend from the ankle to the hoof. The relative length of the pasterns is important, because they're the primary shock absorbers for the concussion that occurs each time the horse takes a step.

If her pasterns are very short, your horse is going to give you a jarring ride, especially at the trot. She'll also be giving herself a jarring ride, and in time she may develop some permanent lameness.

If the pasterns are too long, the ankle may almost sink to the ground when the horse puts a good deal of force on it, such as when she gallops or jumps. This may predispose her to strained tendons or more serious leg injuries.

Still, with light riding, pastern length may not be a problem as long as it's not severely short or long. If it's present on top of a couple of other bad points, it might be enough for you to decide against a horse, but on its own you can usually live with it.

Learn to recognize the ideal feet and legs, but don't necessarily discard a horse just because she's a little less than perfect. If a horse has a fault, ask your veterinarian or a competent horseman if it's one you can live with. Your first horse needs to be sound, not flawless.

What matters is how the horse moves and how she's likely to hold up in the work she'll do for you, not how perfect she looks. Although an unsightly fault will make a horse harder to sell, remember that many faults that could cause serious problems in a racehorse might not cause any in a trail horse.

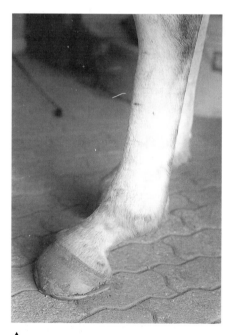

▲

This horse's pasterns are low. They slope too much and have predisposed her to leg injuries.

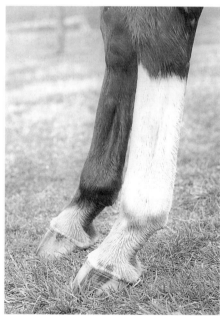

▲

This horse has good conformation of the pasterns.

Tail

You might think that a horse's tail is just a decorative fly swisher; that, other than color and length, it can be disregarded when you evaluate a horse. Alas, this is not quite the case.

If a horse wrings her tail or swings it around a lot while she's being ridden, she's unhappy and nervous. Horses in Western Pleasure or Reining classes are supposed to be relaxed in their work, and judges will penalize a tail wringer. Consequently, in certain show circles, horses' tails are altered to keep them from swishing around during competitions.

An assortment of techniques has been tried to prevent tail swinging. One is nerve blocking tails with an injection, which leaves the tail partially paralyzed. This practice is banned by every major show association, but it still happens. It's usually done at home before the show, often by someone other than a veterinarian. Blocking is expected to last four to six weeks, and some trainers or owners get away with it much of the time because official tail checkers usually appear only at the biggest shows.

I mention this because if a horse's tail is blocked repeatedly, there can be serious consequences. The tail may become crooked, or the horse may suffer permanent partial paralysis that prevents her from swishing flies or even defecating or urinating normally, which can lead to colic. Other horses seem to develop tingling or pain in the top of the tail and become chronic buckers, or may injure themselves in stalls trying to rub sore tails. Some horses may not have medical problems, but if the tail is blocked and discovered at a show, the owner or sometimes the trainer could be banned from showing. If you buy such a horse, you might find yourself stuck with a horse you can't show or sell. Unfortunately, tail blocking is very common.

Whatever horse you're looking at, make sure the tail hangs straight down the middle and can swing any direction. If you want to buy a horse but suspect a problem with her tail, ask a veterinarian during the pre-purchase exam (see page 34) to help you determine if it's a serious problem.

Set Tails

To the uninitiated, the American Saddlebreds seen in the show ring may have peculiar-looking tails. In this breed, the show standard calls for the horses to have set tails. People commonly refer to these as broken tails, but they aren't really broken: A veterinarian has cut the muscles on either side of the top of the tail. The tail is then put in a tail set whenever the horse is in the stall, and this shapes the tail. When the horse is ridden or driven, her tail set is removed and her tail arches into the shape desired for the show ring.

Old Saddlebreds that are no longer put in tail sets have tails that arch a little and flop to one side. These horses have almost full use of their tails; they can swish flies off as well any other animal. You may not approve of tail setting, but the horses can at least use their tails.

Another technique used to get a horse to hold her tail high is called *gingering*. Ginger is placed in the horse's rectum, which burns and causes her to carry her tail high. Gingering is commonly done to Saddlebreds, Morgans, and Arabs in the show ring, although by the breed's own rules it's illegal in Arabs. It's generally never done to Paints, Quarter Horses, or Appaloosas. Most horses react to the ginger merely by carrying their tails high, although some may buck or kick.

This Saddlebred's tail has been set so it arches for the show ring. (Photo by Jamie Donaldson; courtesy of The American Saddlebred Horse Association, Inc.)

Soundness

A sound horse has no defects that impair her ability to do the work you want her to do. Of all the things to be picky about when buying a horse, soundness is one of the most important. The word *soundness* refers primarily to lack of lameness; a sound horse is not lame.

Good feet and legs are especially important, so make sure you have a veterinarian, farrier, or horseman with a good eye for lameness check out any horse before you buy.

If a problem is suspected in the feet, one of these experts may use a hoof tester on the horse. This device applies pressure to different parts of the foot to see if the horse has any sensitivity there, which could indicate a problem. Hoof testers may, for instance, indicate whether the bones that lie inside the foot are painful under pressure. Hoof testers are commonly used to determine sensitivity in the area of the navicular bone. Navicular lameness is an unsoundness serious enough to warrant not buying the horse (see chapter 7).

Sellers often try to gloss over lameness by telling you the horse just had her feet trimmed and is a trifle sore; you should know that competent farriers might occasionally make a horse sore by trimming, but not often. To mask lameness, some unethical sellers might also even administer medication before potential buyers come to see the horse. Examples include phenylbutazone, a pain medication; acepromazine maleate (Acepromazine), a tranquilizer; steroids, anti-inflammatories; or even temporary nerve blocks to the feet.

To avoid these kinds of problems, shop for a horse only from sellers who have a good reputation and are recommended by people you trust. If you're in doubt about a horse's soundness, come back another day and look again. If you're still in doubt, look for another horse.

"Soundness of wind" is an old term used to describe a horse that has no abnormality of the airway that would restrict breathing when the horse works hard. A horse with such an obstruction might be called "wind broken" or nowadays is often called a "roarer," because it makes a loud roaring noise when it breathes. Some roarers can be improved with surgery.

Breed Standards and Conformation Traits

There are no horses with absolutely perfect conformation, but there are horses that come closer to an ideal than others. The ideal differs for each type and breed of horse, and is written down for each breed. This is called the breed standard, and it's determined by experienced people who use the horses of that breed, who know the type of work the horses perform, and who know how they need to be put together to best do the work.

American Saddlebreds, for instance, have very long necks and are selected to be "high headed." Quarter horses should not be high headed. Arabian horses should have flat croups, but Thoroughbreds should not. If you're interested in buying a specific breed of horse, learn all you can about the standard for that breed, especially if you plan to compete.

Shopping for a Horse

A good horse that suits you is wherever you find her. Wonderful horses have come from all sorts of places. A very famous show jumper, Snowman, was purchased out of a truckload of horses on their way to the meatpackers. This doesn't mean, of course, that you should shop for a horse at the meatpacker. The best horse for you may belong to somebody you know who's moving on to something bigger or fancier. You might also find your horse in a professional training barn. Just keep looking until you find the one you want. *Take your time.* That sounds like obvious advice, but if

Soundness Checklist

Examine all the important structures of any horse you're considering. Decide if any faults will interfere with the work you want your horse to do.

✓ Head

✓ Eyes

✓ Mouth

✓ Withers

✓ Legs

✓ Feet

✓ Tail

you're a first-time buyer anxious to have your own horse, it's easy to get so excited you jump the gun and buy on impulse.

Network

Good sources for leads on horses are friends, acquaintances, farriers, and equine veterinarians, because they're the people likely to know horses in your area. If you take riding lessons, your instructor may be an excellent source. Start asking around and you'll quickly develop a network that may help you find a fine horse not yet on the market.

Lesson Barns

Another excellent place to purchase your first horse may be a local lesson barn. If you've been taking lessons, there may be a school horse you already know, like, and would be happy to own. A good school horse is generally quiet and well behaved — the kind perfect for beginning riders. At many lesson barns, school horses are for sale, so don't hesitate to ask the owners if they'd consider selling.

Auctions

One place you should probably *not* buy your first horse, however, is at an auction. There are some people who sell horses at auctions who know more than you do about hiding problems. Horses may be drugged so they look quiet during the sale but wake up later, or they may appear to be sound when they're really quite lame. At auctions, there's no real incentive for a seller to tell the truth. He or she may say things about the horse's wonderful disposition that just aren't true. By the time you find them out the seller will be long gone, with your money. Still, auctions are a good place for you to learn how to look at horses, and to find out what the going price is for the type of horse you want.

Horse Dealers

Dealers handle many horses, and they might have the one you want. As with auctions, approach dealers with caution. Check out the dealer's reputation before you go. If you hear from a reliable source that a dealer is reputable it's probably true. If you have any doubts, err on the side of caution.

Ads

Ads in the paper about horses for sale can lead to interesting adventures. Take a map, some tasty food, and a friend. Make a day out of it and be ready for anything. You may meet wonderful people and the horse of your dreams.

Ads for horses also are appearing these days on the Internet. If you have access to this resource, try searching under the keyword "horses" and you'll be amazed at what you come up with! You might find leads to several horses right in your own area.

Keep in mind that the people running the ads wrote them to make the horse look good. There's often great disparity between the perfect animal described and the one you end up seeing.

Also, Internet prices often seem inflated: The sellers are optimistic. If you find a horse you like, you can always offer less than the asking price. (See page 31 for sample ads.)

Adopting Horses

It's sometimes possible to adopt horses for little or no money. If you're careful, some of the adoptive programs can be great opportunities. Several programs place retired harness racers in pleasure homes. There are also some humane organizations that occasionally place former rescue cases in homes. In these cases, you may have to sign an agreement not to sell the horse, and to allow the humane organization to visit to make sure she's well cared for.

Saving on the purchase price by adopting a horse is nice, but remember that it's the cost of caring for the horse that will be your major expense. In addition, a horse you get for free should be evaluated for temperament, soundness, and suitability just as carefully as one you pay for.

Shopping for a Horse

To shop for a horse:

✓ Network! Spread the word among friends, acquaintances, veterinarians, and farriers.

✓ Check out local lesson barns.

✓ Contact horse dealers recommended by people you trust.

✓ Watch for ads in the paper or on the Internet.

✓ Inquire at horse adoption programs.

Show Up Early

One horseman's trick that will help you more than all the others when you are going to see a horse for sale is to make an appointment, but show up 20 to 30 minutes early. This is a little rude, but the seller will get over it. It will prevent the seller from riding or longeing the horse to exhaustion, then grooming her up nicely before you arrive. By working the horse, the seller could be trying to get the bucks out of her before you have a chance to see how unruly she really is. You want a horse that isn't a saddle bronc.

Some less ethical horse sellers will even sedate an unruly horse or anesthetize the animal's feet to mask lameness.

In short, if the horse you're checking out is being ridden or longed when you arrive, take note: This could be a reasonable situation or a bad one. If you notice needles or syringes near the stall, have a friendly conversation, then remember an appointment you missed, and leave.

What you *should* see if you show up early is a horse being groomed. Ask if you can watch as she's groomed and ridden.

Observe

Here's a suggested procedure for initially checking out a horse for sale:

1. Look at the horse and gather your first impression.
2. Watch the horse's behavior while she's being groomed and tacked up. Notice if she is broke to tie or trained to stand in cross-ties calmly. Does she bite or kick when her girth is fastened? A horse that really resents the girth may be ill mannered, but more likely has a sore back. Often such a horse actually has sore hocks as well.
3. Watch carefully while the rider mounts. Does the horse stand quietly to be mounted? A little movement might be acceptable, but if the horse rushes off before the rider is near the saddle, this may signal a problem you don't want.
4. Check out soundness. It will probably take a veterinarian or experienced farrier to detect subtle lameness, but if you think the horse isn't moving quite right, she probably isn't. Remember, soundness of movement is the most important thing to look for. Steer clear of lame horses.
5. Ask for the horse to be ridden the way you plan to ride her. Ask to see her walk, trot, and canter in both directions. The horse should be willing to go toward and away from the barn quietly. She should stop when asked, and move forward willingly.

    If the seller says the horse willingly crosses creeks, ask him or her to take you to a creek and demonstrate. If the seller says the horse is a great jumper, and this is something you want to do, ask him or her to jump the horse.

Ride

If the horse up to this point appears safe to ride, ask if you can ride her once she's reasonably warmed up, but not exhausted. If you don't yet have much riding practice, take along a more experienced riding friend to do the following:

1. Notice if the horse is as well mannered when you or your friend mount as she was for the seller. Does she stand quietly and patiently?

2. Ride the horse. Listen to any instructions the seller offers, however. If he or she tells you that the horse likes very light leg pressure, ride the horse that way, but find out what happens if you touch her with just a bit more leg, and then a little more. Ask the horse to walk, trot, and canter. Does she do so as well for you or your friend as for the seller? Is she equally good going both directions? (Some horses travel and behave much better one way than the other. This could indicate a training problem, a lameness problem, or a vision problem; most often it's a training problem.) Can she travel in a comfortable circle while maintaining speed? Will she slow down easily and halt quietly for you?

3. Trot the horse on a circle; this is often the best place to see or feel lameness. Does she seem sound?

4. Ask the horse to do a wide variety of reasonable things. What happens when she's ridden away from the barn? What happens when she's ridden away from other horses, or near other horses? Does she act up? What happens when she's pointed back toward the barn? Does she automatically increase speed and pull like a train? A barn sour horse can be a big problem, and dangerous. Look instead for a horse that's comfortable in all reasonable situations.

5. If you have enough riding experience, ride the horse outside the ring (or have your more experienced friend do so) and see if she remains calm. There are some horses that have been ridden in the ring all their lives. Some don't even really know how to steer when they're away from walls or fences.

Double-Check Ground Manners

Don't forget to check out ground manners yourself.

✓ Is the horse well behaved while you dismount?

✓ Lead her around by the reins. Does she lead nicely?

✓ Have someone hold the horse while you loosen, then tighten, the girth or cinch a bit. Does she tolerate this well?

✓ See if the horse will lift each foot for you as if you're about to pick out her feet.

✓ Can you touch her on the head and ears, or is she head-shy?

◄

When you're checking out a horse, don't forget to check ground manners. Will the horse politely let you pick up her feet? Can you touch her ears?

Trailering

Ask the seller if the horse loads well onto a trailer, and have the seller demonstrate the horse's willingness to load. Many horse buyers don't do this, but I think it's important. You need to have a horse that you can take where you want, especially if you plan to show. In addition, teaching a chronic bad loader how to load well and safely is beyond the patience and ability of most beginners.

You should also try to load the horse yourself after the seller has shown you how. If there's some ritual to loading her that you're going to be saddled with forever (e.g., the horse only loads on the left side of the trailer, and two people have to stand beside her to get her on), now is the time to find out if you can live with it.

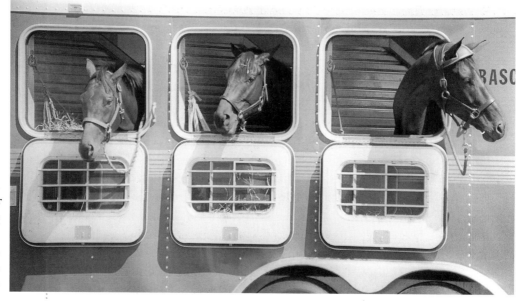

▶
It's wise to find out if the horse you want to buy hauls well. These three seem perfectly content! (This trailer is parked.)

Think It Over

If you like most of what you've seen, don't buy the horse, go home and think it over. It's too easy to get caught up in the moment and make a hasty purchase — and a mistake.

If you do decide to buy this horse, make it clear that your purchase is dependent upon the results of a prepurchase examination conducted by a veterinarian (see page 34).

What Price to Pay?

The cost of horses varies so widely that it's impossible to tell you what you should or shouldn't pay for one. Generally a purebred, which you'll learn more about in the next chapter (see page 59) is going to cost more than a crossbred. An old horse is going to cost less than a younger horse in her prime, but a green horse may cost even less, because she lacks training. A horse with a show record is going to cost more than one that's been used strictly for pleasure riding.

What's important is that you establish what you can afford to pay before you even begin to shop. When you find a horse you like that's in your price range, ask a knowledgeable horseman you know to give an opinion about whether the asking price seems reasonable. By looking at many horses, you'll also develop a feel yourself for what's reasonable and what's not.

To give you a rough idea of how much prices can vary among horses, I've pulled some sample ads with prices from an East Coast horse publication.

Strawberry Roan, Appy mare 13 yrs. old, goes English/Western. 15h. No time to ride. Great pleasure horse. $1,800.

Thoroughbred Mare, 8 yrs., 15h, Chestnut. Trail rides, pleasure. Owned by veterinarian. $600.

Quarter Horse gelding, 15.3h, Western/English pleasure. Great on trails, great family horse or first horse. Real gentleman. $2,500.

Gray Thoroughbred mare, 10 yrs., 16h. Placed well in hunter, jumper events. Loads, clips, good on trails. $4,500.

Bay mare, 8 yrs., 14.1h, very quiet, hacks beautifully, trail rides, jumps 2'6". $4,200.

Talented 7 yr. old dark bay w/white, 16h, started over fences. Owners don't have time for him. $10,000.

Get a Contract

Be sure to obtain a sales contract when you buy your horse. It should clearly identify the horse and state the purchase price, any special payment provisions, and any stipulations — such as that the sale is contingent on the veterinary pre-purchase examination.

Vices

Vices are habits or behaviors that are undesirable. Some are just annoying, but some are dangerous, so watch for them in any horse you consider buying.

Cribbing

The horse puts her top teeth on a rigid surface, arches her neck, and makes noises by sucking in air. This vice is annoying because horses that crib tend to destroy fence boards and stall doors. Some horsemen believe that cribbing also predisposes a horse to colic, although this is controversial. Cribbing is virtually impossible to correct once the habit is established, but there are special collars that apply pressure to the neck or temple muscles when the horse tries to crib, which may help discourage this behavior. If you find a horse that's good in every other way and has no history of colic, cribbing may be a perfectly acceptable vice, if you can tolerate the noise. Some boarding barns will not accept cribbers.

Weaving

A weaver rocks back and forth from one front leg to the other, usually at the front of the stall. This is a vice that is potentially contagious; another horse watches a weaver and begins to weave. Then another horse that can see the new weaver begins weaving, and so it goes. Some chronic weavers actually make themselves lame by repeating the weaving endlessly.

This vice is annoying, difficult to correct, and usually signals a nervous horse. In other cases, though, the weaving horse is fine in every other regard, and the solution is simply to keep her outdoors most of the time, because most horses that weave do so only when in their stalls. Whether you should buy a horse that weaves, then, may depend on how you plan to keep her. If you'll board her at a place where horses are stalled most of the time, a weaver may not be your best choice.

Biting

Some horses get nippy about one thing or another, such as having their girth tightened, but don't nip or bite at other times; some horses may bite anytime you do something they don't like. A little nip in the air when the girth is fastened is often no cause for alarm, and this is the kind of problem that might be cured with consistent handling and patience. But any horse that really tries to bite at any time is potentially dangerous, especially around small children. You'll have to decide how serious the nipping or biting problem is, and whether you think you can handle and correct it.

Kicking

Most horses occasionally kick up their heels at other horses while they're out playing in the field. Some horses kick at the walls of their stalls but never at people. Some kick at people and at other horses, even while you're riding them. Any horse that kicks at people should be avoided; if you're a beginner, also try to avoid a horse that kicks at other horses while mounted. Children should never handle or ride kickers.

Rearing

This vice is extremely dangerous. As I mentioned before, a horse can rear high enough that she falls over backward on top of you. Do not buy a horse that rears. This vice is completely unacceptable, particularly for a novice.

Shying

Most horses will shy at something because of fear. A usually docile horse that's unafraid of tractors, trucks, and bicycles may be fearful of a plastic bag blowing along the ground. A horse that doesn't mind plastic bags might find a bicycle terrifying.

What you want to avoid is the horse that shies at many things easily, because that's when the behavior becomes potentially dangerous. With time and consistent handling, the fearful horse can learn to better cope with the world, but the learning phase may be risky for the rider, especially a beginner. Opt for a horse that's calm and unlikely to be alarmed by the things you'll encounter while riding.

Barn Sour

A barn sour horse persistently tries to avoid leaving the barn; if she's away from home, she quickly tries to drag the rider back to the barn. This vice is potentially dangerous, especially around children, who may not be able to control the horse. Still, with consistent work the barn sour horse often will improve.

Pulling Back

The horse is not broke to tie and suddenly and violently pulls back when tied. This is another potentially dangerous vice. Horses can be taught to tie, but a fearful horse with a bad history about tying is too much of a risk for beginners or children. There are many horses out there broke to tie well. Retraining a horse that pulls back is not something that a novice should try. Evaluate a trainer's technique carefully before you let him or her try to "cure" the horse. With many techniques, the horse could get hurt.

Veterinary Check

Once you think you've found a safe, sound, and suitable horse, have her checked over by a veterinarian before you buy. This is called a pre-purchase examination. It's money well spent, because it may prevent you from arriving home with a horse you can't ride and can't sell and that also happens to be expensive to keep.

Veterinary medicine is specialized today, just like human medicine, so you'll want an equine practitioner, not the local doctor who treats cats and dogs. In some places, there just aren't very many equine veterinarians. If this is the case, it might be worth your while to arrange to have the horse hauled to an equine clinic, where a veterinarian who specializes in horses can do the prepurchase examination. Ideally, the veterinarian you select should not be the one the seller uses. Such a veterinarian might be hesitant to openly tell you about anything he or she finds wrong, for fear of alienating the seller (who is her or her client). Neither should this person be a good friend of one or both sides in the sale. If the veterinarian is completely neutral, you'll be more likely to get a fair assessment. On the other hand, there are veterinarians who know the seller well, routinely conduct prepurchase examinations for buyers, and do a fine job. You'll have to make some judgments about the integrity of the seller and veterinarian you're dealing with.

The Prepurchase Examination

Different veterinarians go about the prepurchase examination in different ways. It would be wise to let the veterinarian know anything about the horse you're especially concerned with, and ask ahead of time what the examination will cost.

The veterinarian is likely to check the eyes with an ophthalmoscope, and check out the horse's mouth. Ask the doctor to estimate the horse's age by her teeth to see if it's close to the age the seller told you. Aging a horse

---

Ask the Veterinarian

Many of these questions are best asked when the seller of the horse isn't present, if possible.

✓ How old is the horse?

✓ Did you find any problems?

✓ How is her vision?

✓ Do you think she's physically able to do what I want her to?

✓ Do you think she's suited to do what I want her to?

✓ What are the results of X rays, if taken?

✓ Do you suspect any drugging?

✓ Are there any other tests you'd suggest?

---

by her teeth is an inexact science, but the veterinarian's estimate should be within a year of what you've been told. Be aware that if a horse is a cribber (which I explained earlier in this chapter on page 32), she may have worn her teeth in a way that makes it hard to age her.

The veterinarian also is likely to listen to the horse's heart and lungs carefully, and take her temperature, since a fever could indicate some sort of infectious disease.

The horse's legs should be examined very closely; most veterinarians will want to use hoof testers on the feet to see if there's any sensitivity that might indicate a problem. All veterinarians should ask you to jog the horse so they can watch how she goes and try to pick up any signs of lameness. The doctor should ask you to mount, since some lamenesses will show up only when there's weight on the horse. After you ride, the veterinarian may also listen for respiratory noises that are only present when the horse works.

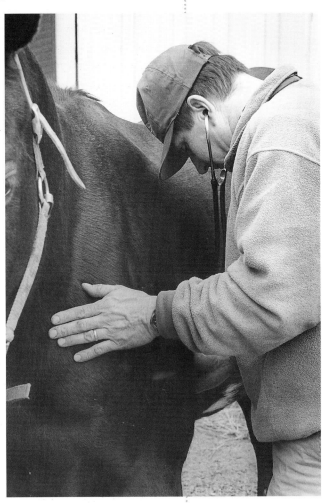

Some veterinarians will insist on X rays of the feet or other joints, especially if the horse will be used for more strenuous sports such as jumping; others don't recommend X rays for a horse to be used as a pleasure mount unless a problem is suspected.

Unless the horse has had a recent Coggins test, blood will be drawn for one. This is a test for equine infectious anemia (EIA) and it's required by law in many areas. (See chapter 7 for more on EIA.)

▲
It's a good idea to have a veterinarian examine any horse you want to buy.

You should be checking out horses only from reputable sellers whom you trust. If you're not sure, you might want to ask the veterinarian if the blood should be checked for the presence of tranquilizers or painkillers. It's not always possible to test for everything you want, and it's often expensive, so discuss this with the veterinarian first.

Remember that veterinarians aren't perfect, and they aren't prophets. In most cases, they can't tell what will go wrong with a horse down the road. They can inform you of any potential problems they see the day of the prepurchase examination, and explain what those problems may or may not mean. Then you'll have to decide for yourself if you can live with whatever faults or defects the veterinarian has found.

Most often, the doctor will find some things that are less than perfect; these are gray areas. In these cases, it's wise to ask many questions. A good way to phrase a question at this point is, "If you were considering this horse, what would you do?" For liability reasons, some veterinarians will not make absolute judgments and will flat-out decline to tell you whether they think a horse is suitable for you, but others will.

Try to establish a good, professional relationship by being courteous, but don't be intimidated or afraid to ask questions. You're paying for the exam, so go ahead and ask. Some excellent veterinarians aren't great talkers, and you might have to pry a bit to get the information you want. Do try to ask pertinent questions without taking all day, and listen carefully to what the veterinarian tells you.

If the seller is present, be respectful. Don't place the seller in an uncomfortable position in front of the veterinarian. If there's something you need to know but don't want to ask in front of the seller, take the veterinarian aside if you can and ask, or call him or her later to discuss the situation.

Prepurchase Examination

Different veterinarians go about conducting prepurchase examinations differently, but here are some items they're likely to check out:

✓ Mouth	✓ Heart	✓ Feet
✓ Teeth (and age)	✓ Lungs	✓ Tail
✓ Eyes	✓ Joints	✓ Movement

Some veterinarians may recommend X rays of the horse's feet routinely; others only do so if a problem is suspected or if the horse will be used for more strenuous sports.

You may also want to ask the veterinarian if blood tests are necessary. Some horses may need a Coggins. Some veterinarians may advise a complete blood count (CBC), or a check for the presence of drugs such as tranquilizers, painkillers, or steroids.

3

Breeds of Horses

There's no one breed that's better than all the others. Of course, everyone who likes a particular breed best will argue with this statement. For your first horse, however, think in terms of buying the best individual horse for you, whatever breed he happens to be.

There may be special situations. For instance, if all your friends go to Appaloosa shows and that's what you want to do, too, then you may want to buy an Appaloosa. Otherwise, don't be too specific about the breed you want: This will give you many more horses to look at. And the more horses you have to look at, the greater your chances of finding the one that's right for you.

Still, there are some characteristics associated with specific breeds, and it may help you narrow down your search if you know these in advance. Thus I'll list here the breeds you're most likely to run across (and a few that are fairly rare, but interesting), as well as some general points about each breed.

Breeds with Standard Gaits

The breeds of horses mentioned below have three standard gaits: the walk, the trot, and the canter. In Western parlance, these gaits are called the walk, the jog, and the lope.

Appaloosa

These are wildly colored, spotted horses developed by the Nez Perce tribe of Native Americans. Appaloosas, commonly referred to as Appys, come in two major genetic color patterns.

Leopard Appaloosas are spotted all over like dalmatian dogs or, of course, leopards. The background color of the horse is close to white and the spots may be black, bay, rusty red, or even Palomino colored. The eyes of the horse may be brown or blue (this latter is referred to as a glass eye).

The second color pattern is the blanket Appaloosa. These horses have spots in a "blanket"-shaped area, usually confined to the rump. The rest of the horse may be black or gray (although gray is not considered desirable, because it's associated with fading color); red, dun, or Palomino; or something in between.

All Appaloosas must have mottled skin and mottling around the eye. No two are identical. Just when you think you understand what an Appaloosa looks like, it gets confusing. There are now registerable Appaloosas, in fact, that have no spots at all. This stems from the fact that one solid-colored parent, when bred to a colored horse, may produce either colored or solid foals. Therefore the registry decided that it was foolish not to register the solid foals at least as "breeding stock."

Appaloosas are often wonderful athletes with excellent dispositions. There has been some concern that eye problems may be more common in Appys than in other breeds. Little scientific documentation of this exists, but a higher incidence of eye problems has been noted anecdotally by some veterinarians with many years of experience, along with some Appaloosa owners and horse dealers. It's certainly not a reason to take an Appaloosa off your list of candidates; simply be aware of these potential problems and have the horse's eyes checked out carefully.

Arabian

Arabians are probably the most classically beautiful horses. They're known for their dished faces, huge, soft eyes, and floaty gaits. Arabs come in almost any solid color you can imagine, as well as roans and rose-grays.

In general, Arabs aren't large horses. They're known for being spirited and for having great stamina. This stamina, however, can work against you if you're not an experienced rider: If a spirited Arab is full of himself one cool windy day, he could be too much for you to handle.

Arabs are the breed of choice for competitive trail and endurance riding. Those who want to show will find that there are plenty of Arabian shows almost everywhere. If you want a beautiful, sensitive horse with great spirit and endurance, an Arab could be for you.

Arabs are not especially well suited to jumping. The same conformation that gives the breed beautiful, floaty gaits also inhibits the Arabian's ability to use his hind end in a way that enables him to jump well. An Arab can

easily get over fences, up to about 3 feet, if sound and properly trained —
just not with the form that show hunter judges like to see.

Arabs aren't considered the breed of choice in dressage shows, where
Warmbloods prevail, or in Western shows, which are open to all breeds but
where Quarter Horses seem to be preferred. If you want to be a rising star
in these shows, it could be hard to reach your goal on an Arab, even if the
horse does the work brilliantly.

Be careful of people who want you to invest large quantities of money
in Arabian horses. In recent decades, the market for Arabs has fluctuated
wildly. Some horses that were bought for fortunes were later sold for next
to nothing. Buy the right horse for you because you like him, not because
of his investment value.

Miniature Horses

There are two main organizations that register miniature horses. The
American Miniature Horse Association will accept for registration only
horses that are the offspring of registered parents, and that meet a height
requirement. An adult mini may be no larger than 34 inches. The American
Miniature Horse Registry also will accept only horses of registered parents,
but has two height divisions. In the first or "A" division, the horses may be
no larger than 34 inches as adults. In the second or "B" division, the horses
may be no larger than 38 inches as adults.

Miniature horses are the only breed that's not measured to the highest
point of the withers: The horses are correctly measured to the last hair of
the mane.

Everybody knows that miniature horses are too small for adults to ride,
but quite a few people think they can start their children riding on minis.
This isn't a very workable idea, either. The horses are so small that they're
quickly outgrown by children.

Still, minis are great little driving animals for adults or children. They
can easily pull good-size adults in carts, there are many driving classes at
their shows, and there's even a miniature racing association.

A well-chosen mini mare or gelding is also an excellent choice for
someone with physical limitations who wants to enjoy horses: Most mini
carts can be adapted to handle wheelchairs. There are many retired adults
owning and showing minis who like horses but don't want to deal with big
horses anymore. And there are plenty of mini owners who simply enjoy the
horses as companion animals and don't drive or show them.

When choosing a mini, be careful to check out his mouth. Peculiar
bites are relatively common, and could be important if your horse is going
to wear a bridle to drive. Be careful of horses that are proportioned incorrectly. If the head seems too big and the body is noticeably longer than it is
high, the horse may be a dwarf. This is a heritable genetic deformity that's
not desirable in breeding animals.

Minis come in all solid colors as well as Pintos and Appaloosas.

Morgan

Morgans are an all-purpose American breed developed in Colonial New England. Today, they remain common in New England and are popular in California as well as in pockets throughout the rest of the United States.

Morgans are solid, usually dark-colored horses. They may have blazes or stockings. Morgans make excellent driving and pleasure horses. Be aware that they usually aren't very big, but are sturdy and athletic, and are famous for having very long life spans. Morgan brood mares are often having foals well into their 20s.

In general, Morgans are even tempered. A well-chosen Morgan could be a good horse for many beginners, but in some parts of the United States they are scarce and may cost more than what a first-time buyer can afford. Depending on where you live, you might have to travel to find the Morgan you want.

Mustang

Most people think of Mustangs as wild horses. Technically, these horses are feral animals, which means they are free-running escapees or offspring of escapees of domestic horse stock.

Mustangs have been running free in the West since shortly after the first horses arrived with the Conquistadores. Even though they aren't true wild horses from a technical, zoological point of view, from a handling point of view they most certainly are wild.

The Bureau of Land Management offers a wild-horse adoption program for Mustangs, but adoption isn't a good idea for a beginning rider. Only experienced horsemen should take on a wild horse. If a well-broke Mustang comes up for sale and you like him, however, there's no reason not to give him a try.

Mustangs are inclined to be small, wiry, and tough, but they are athletes. One of the top competitive trail horses in the country in recent years was a Mustang mare. Mustangs come in nearly any color, solid or Pinto.

Paints and Pintos

Paints and Pintos are spotted horses with large blocks of color rather than the small, dalmatian-like spots seen on Appaloosas. The difference between Paints and Pintos has to do with the organizations that register them.

Paints might be thought of as Western-type spotted horses. To be registered as a Paint, the horse must have two registered Paint parents, or one Paint parent and one Quarter Horse parent, or one Paint parent and one Thoroughbred parent. New rules designed to benefit Paint racing allow the registration of a horse with two Thoroughbred parents. But whatever his parentage, the horse must be of qualifying color. If he doesn't have any spots, he isn't registerable.

bay overo

PAINT ▶

*Photo courtesy of American
Paint Horse Association*

sorrel tobiano

▲ RACKING HORSE

Photo by Sandra Hall; courtesy of Racking Horse Breeders' Association of America

▼ MISSOURI FOX TROTTER

Photo courtesy of Valley View Farm, Hastings, MN

▲ ROCKY MOUNTAIN HORSE

*Photo courtesy of the Rocky Mountain
Horse Association*

FRIESIAN ▶

*Photo by Alger Meekma;
courtesy of Friesian Horse
Association of North America*

TULSA, OK 1996

▲ **PALOMINO**

*Photo courtesy of Palomino Horse
Breeders of America, Inc.*

▼ **ANGLO-ARAB**

*Photo by Lela Feucua; courtesy
of Zrurik Farm, Reno, NV*

▲ TRAKEHNER

Photo courtesy of American Trakehner Association

▼ STANDARDBRED

Photo courtesy of United States Trotting Association

▲ HANOVERIAN

Photo by Scarlett Pflugrad; courtesy of American Hanoverian Horse Society

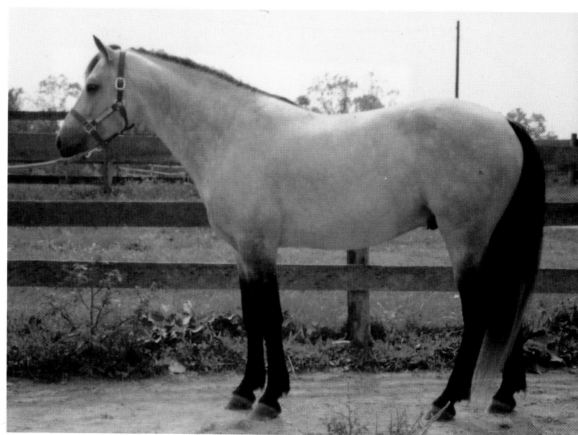

CONNEMARA ▶
PONY

Photo courtesy of American Connemara Pony Society

◀ **ARABIAN**
Photo by Jeff Janson; courtesy of International Arabian Horse Association

▼ **MUSTANG**
New England Stock

▲ Shetland Pony

*Photo by Toni Mayr; courtesy of Singletree Farm,
Rocky Ridge, MD*

▼ Pony of the Americas

*Photo courtesy of the Pony
of the Americas Club, Inc.*

▲ MORGAN

*Photo courtesy of American
Morgan Horse Association*

▼ PASO FINO

*Photo by Larry Williams; courtesy
of Paso Fino Horse Association, Inc.*

TENNESSEE WALKER ▲
*Photo ©1997 by Stuart
Vesty; courtesy of Tennessee
Walking Horse Breeders' and
Exhibitors' Association,
Lewisburg, TN*

SADDLEBRED ▶
*Photo by Jamie
Donaldson; courtesy of
The American Saddlebred
Horse Association, Inc.*

▲ PINTO

Photo courtesy of Pinto Horse Association of America, Inc.

◀ HACKNEY PONY

Photo courtesy of Hackney World

▲ Haflinger Pony
© Dusty L. Perin

▼ Thoroughbred
© Dusty L. Perin

▲ **GRADE HORSE**
Lisa Helfert

◀ **WELSH PONY**
© *Dusty L. Perin*

AMERICAN QUARTER HORSE

Painting by Orren Mixer. An artist's conception of the ideal American Quarter Horse; courtesy of AQHA.

Pintos, on the other hand, are horses of any breed that have qualifying color. Therefore you might have a Pinto American Saddlebred, or a Pinto Shetland pony; neither could qualify as a Paint, however, because the Paint registry doesn't accept these breeds. It's common to find Paints that have also been registered as Pintos. This doubles the number of shows the horses can enter.

Paints and Pintos can be quite dazzling to look at, but if you intend to show in the hunter ring, you may find that the judges dislike wild colors.

These horses come in two basic genetic color patterns: tobiano and overo. Tobianos have big blocks of color next to the white. A famous tobiano from yesteryear that you might have seen on *The Lone Ranger* TV series was Tonto's horse, Scout. In general — and this is very general, because no two are quite the same — a tobiano has a face marked like any other breed of horse. It might be solid colored or have a blaze or a star. Usually, all the legs on a tobiano are white, at least below the hocks and knees, and they usually have color on one or both flanks. The tails of tobianos are often two colors.

The other, somewhat more exotic pattern is the overo. Overos generally have ragged blotches of color along the spine and the belly, with ragged blotches of white on the sides. Overos' tails are usually one color. Some people find it useful to remember that overos have color that goes *over* the back. Others find this description confusing, because the horses vary so much. The face of an overo may have a wild unusual blaze, or it may have a blaze so wide that the white goes beyond one or both eyes. Such a horse is known as a bald-faced horse, and he'll often have blue eyes.

A few horses have color patterns with characteristics of both the tobiano and the overo. These are known in the Paint registry as toveros.

If you have British or older American books, you may run into the terms *piebald* and *skewbald.* These are color terms. A piebald horse is a black and white Pinto (or Paint); a skewbald is any other color Pinto (or Paint), but most often a red and white one.

Palomino

Palominos are a color, not a true breed. There are Palomino Quarter Horses and Palomino Paso Finos. An association sanctions shows for Palomino horses. If you're mad for golden horses, there's no reason you shouldn't own a Palomino. Don't be dazzled by the gold, however, when looking at any horse: Color should be low on your list of priorities. Don't forget to consider conformation, soundness, and temperament!

Quarter Horses

Quarter Horses are by far the most common breed of horses in the country: There are about ten Quarter Horses for every one of the next most common breed. Quarter Horses are often the breed of choice for first-time buyers, because they're generally docile and can be found in any price range.

Remember, however, that just because the breed is supposed to be quiet doesn't mean every individual will be. A Quarter Horse with a bad training history can be as difficult as any other kind of horse.

Quarter Horses can make excellent pleasure animals, but make sure that during the prepurchase veterinary exam the feet are examined closely. Navicular disease seems to be common in this breed. This is a degeneration of the navicular bone, a little pyramid-shaped bone in the middle of the foot. (Learn more about this disease in chapter 7.) There are plenty of Quarter Horses out there without navicular disease — it's just something to have checked out before you buy.

Appendix Horse

Appendix Horse is a Quarter Horse registry term referring to a horse with one Quarter Horse parent and one Thoroughbred parent. Such an animal may be shown in all Quarter Horse shows, but if he's going to be bred, either he must be bred to a Quarter Horse that's not an Appendix Horse (these horses are called permanent registered Quarter Horses) or, before he's bred, he must earn a specific number of points in Quarter Horse shows or races. Thus, it's possible for an Appendix Horse, which is itself half Thoroughbred, to earn enough show points to be bred to a Thoroughbred. Logic would tell you the resulting foal would be 75 percent Thoroughbred, but it could be registered as an Appendix Quarter Horse. This can go on for many generations. For this reason, some people grumble that there's more Thoroughbred blood in some bloodlines than Quarter Horse.

For your first horse, though, family tree should not be as important to you as soundness and behavior. Whether he's an Appendix Horse or a permanent registered Quarter Horse with nary a Thoroughbred in his pedigree is irrelevant. The only thing that matters is whether he's the right horse for you.

Thoroughbred

A Thoroughbred is a breed unto itself, with pedigrees that trace back to the 1700s. Thoroughbreds were created to be racing animals. They have tremendous speed over distance, and are famous for their heart, or courage.

Thoroughbreds are usually characterized as being hot tempered, nervous, skittish animals. They certainly can be, but this is often a product of their training, or lack of training, not a result of innate nervousness.

Many Thoroughbreds used for racing have only been trained to accept a light rider, have a vague idea of steering, and bolt out of the starting gate and run. When their racing career ends they go out into the world of riding horses knowing nearly nothing about how to behave under saddle. They're usually extremely sensitive. Because they've been bred and trained to run, they tend to run from any new, scary experience. When you pull on the reins of a race-trained horse while he's running, he'll run faster, not slower, because that's what happens on the track. To slow down the jockey must sit up and bring the horse to the outside of the track, which certainly isn't the way average pleasure riders ride.

As someone about to acquire your first horse, you want an animal trained the way you were taught to ride. In short, stay away from horses that have recently come off the track. It's also possible that a horse taken off the track wasn't just too slow or too old for this sport; he may have an injury that isn't readily obvious.

More Thoroughbreds are being bred today for the show ring or hunt field, however, and they aren't trained the way racehorses are trained. As one experienced trainer put it, "I believe these horses are smarter, quicker to learn, and more eager to please their riders than any other breed." This kind of Thoroughbred just might make a fine first horse if he meets all your other requirements.

Some Thoroughbreds have also come off the track to be retrained by careful and knowledgeable people. Such horses are appropriate if you have some riding experience.

If you're considering a Thoroughbred, consider the horse's background and your own level of skill.

Thoroughbred or Purebred?

Nonhorsemen often confuse the term *Thoroughbred* with the word *purebred*. The former indicates a specific breed of horse — a Thoroughbred — just as the word *poodle* indicates a specific breed of dog. You can have a purebred Thoroughbred, meaning a horse that's 100 percent Thoroughbred, or a purebred Arabian, but you can't have a Thoroughbred Arabian or a Thoroughbred Quarter Horse, or a Thoroughbred poodle for that matter, because a Thoroughbred is a different breed of horse altogether.

Warmbloods

Warmbloods are not one breed of horse; instead the name is given to a group of different breeds vaguely similar in type, especially those that come from Europe.

Warmbloods were created largely by the military, which crossed true draft horses with Thoroughbreds and Arabs and then selected only the offspring with the best conformation and gaits. Draft horses, which are very large, are known as "cold blooded." This doesn't mean they're ruthless killers; rather, it means they're slow moving, not flighty, and not terribly sensitive. Hot-blooded horses are just the opposite. The two breeds that are officially (as decreed by tradition) regarded as hot blooded are Arabians and Thoroughbreds.

Careful, selective breeding of Warmbloods has been going on since the 1700s, and has resulted in individuals that are very true to type and consistent in their gaits and movement. Warmbloods have recently become quite fashionable in the United States. They're often huge; they're traditionally dark colored without much white or gray, although recently some Pinto Warmbloods have made a splash in American show rings.

The popularity of Warmbloods is understandable. They're magnificent movers. Their gaits are correct and their stride is long, powerful, and beautiful. And despite their larger-than-usual size, Warmbloods can be athletic. They're commonly seen in dressage shows at the highest levels, and are making their mark in hunter shows as well. A number of Warmbloods are among the best show jumpers in the world; the animals are also common in combined driving events. They're too big and heavy, however, for Western riding events.

Warmbloods can be difficult to handle. As a rule, they aren't nervous or flighty, but can be incredibly stubborn. Some of them are prone to temper tantrums that can be frightening and even dangerous. If your Warmblood has these sorts of problems, get help from a professional who has worked with Warmbloods and knows how to handle them.

Because Warmbloods are all the rage these days, the prices are often outrageous. Still, the fashion runs to large horses, so smaller Warmbloods can sometimes be found for sale at good prices.

If you're considering one of these breeds for your first horse, make certain you acquire a mature animal well beyond the age of foolishness; he should also have served someone else reliably. It should be noted that in Europe, many of these horses are not even started under saddle until they're five or six years old. They're ready to go to work at this point and to have a long, useful working life. The American technique of feeding growing horses massive amounts of protein and every feed supplement on the market, then starting them to work when they're two, can take its toll on the soundness of any horses, but especially on large, slow-maturing ones. Make sure that during the prepurchase check, your veterinarian closely examines and X-rays the hocks. More than a few of these Warmblood horses develop hock or other joint problems even before they're put to work.

Here are some breeds of Warmbloods.

Trakehner

The Trakehner was developed about 1720 in Trakehenen, Germany. Trakehners are thought to be the lightest boned of the Warmbloods and often served as military officers' horses.

In the United States, there are two associations that register Trakehners. The American Trakehner Association works with the horses that can trace their ancestry, faultlessly, to Germany; the North American Trakehner Association registers Trakehner horses that may have ancestors from Poland. One of America's great Olympic jumpers, Abdullah, was a German Trakehner originally imported to Canada *in utero*, which means he got here as part of a package with his pregnant mother.

Hanoverian

Hanoverians are from Hanover, Germany. In general, this is a slightly heavier breed of horse than the Trakehner. Hanoverians are brilliant movers, often seen in dressage shows.

Holsteiner

Holsteiners are among the heaviest of the German Warmbloods. Of course, individuals may be far lighter than the average. There are fewer Holsteiners in this country than Trakehners or Hanoverians, and they excel in big jumper and dressage shows.

Friesian (or Fresian)

An ancient breed from the Netherlands that is not a true Warmblood is the Friesian. These horses have been documented in history since about the year A.D. 150, and it was an old breed even then. Friesians are large, strong-boned horses that have been noted since ancient times for their gentleness. They carried knights to war in the Crusades. They've been used as coach horses, farm horses, and riding horses. They're always black, and may be anywhere from about 15h to about 17h in height. They're known to be wonderful movers.

This is a breed that's small in numbers with a studbook still managed by the Dutch government, which is extraordinarily picky about the horses used for breeding. Only those with the best physical traits and perfect dispositions are bred. There are just 50 breeding stallions in the world. It's easy to fall in love with these magnificent black horses, but expect their prices to reflect their rarity.

Dutch Warmblood

One other European breed that has made a big impression in the world of horse shows has quite a different history from other Warmbloods. It's the Dutch Warmblood, which was created after World War II in the Netherlands by a tiny group of horse breeders who knew what they wanted to produce — a great breed of sport horse. They set about it in a purposeful way, carefully selecting only stallions and mares that had every one of the desired qualities. Of the foals they produced, they kept only the very best. The breed boasts an impressive number of great jumping and dressage horses.

There has recently been a spate of Pinto Dutch Warmbloods in the United States, most of them tracing to one very correct and wildly colored stallion. The fashion of solid-colored horses, especially in the dressage ring, seems to be changing.

Other Breeds of Warmbloods

These include the Oldenburg and Westphalian, which are also breeds from Germany. From France comes the Selle Français, a breed that has produced a number of world-class show jumpers. The ancestry of the Selle

Français includes some French Trotter, a distant kin to our Standardbred, as well as Thoroughbred and Arab, and little if any Draft blood. Strictly speaking, the Selle Français isn't a Warmblood, but in casual conversation most Americans lump it into this group, to the annoyance of the French.

If you're shopping for a Warmblood, you may also come across Swedish Warmbloods, which are best known for their brilliance in dressage, although some certainly compete in other sports.

American Warmbloods

If by definition a Warmblood is a Draft Horse crossed with a Thoroughbred or Arab, why can't the crossing be done in this country so we Americans get some of the glory? The process has in fact been tried here and there, and some pretty good individual sport horses have come out of it. However, the problems come in consistency of type over time. The first-generation crosses are sometimes just what you want, but the second generation may produce horses much more like one side of the family tree than the other. Remember, the Europeans have been breeding Warmbloods for 250 years (in the case of the Friesian, for nearly 2,000 years), and selecting only the best.

In the United States owners, rather than highly trained and critical military officers, decide what horses to breed. There is therefore little impartial selection; few horses are eliminated from the breeding herd, no matter what their faults. Still, you might find a good American Warmblood. In standard, slightly snobby, horse lingo it would be called an American Sport Horse or a name derived from some form of the family tree, such as a Thorough-Dale (Thoroughbred x Clydesdale).

Crossbreds

Crossbred horses are common. Sometimes the horse was bred on purpose out of two selected parental breeds. Sometimes two horses simply got together when they weren't expected to, and the result was a crossbred. There are a few breeds crossed frequently enough that the cross has earned a name of its own, even though it isn't truly a breed.

If you run across a horse said to be an Anglo-Arab, you've found a horse that's half Thoroughbred and half Arab. Similarly, an Anglo-Morgan is half Thoroughbred and half Morgan. (If you're being fussy about the term *Anglo,* this designates an English Thoroughbred only; if you're more like the masses, *Anglo* can mean any Thoroughbred in a crossbred horse.) A Mor-Ab is a Morgan x Arab cross.

The International Arabian Horse Association also registers half Arabs. It doesn't matter what the non-Arab half is; if your horse is registered with the association, he can compete in its shows.

Recently, a new crossbred has been developed especially for the show ring: the National Show Horse. These horses are half American Saddlebred and half Arabian. To be registered in the National Show Horse

Registry, the sire must first be registered, at significant expense. This is important, because these horses are now quite fashionable in the show ring. You might decide you want to own one. If you find an animal that's the right cross but unregistered, and you're unaware of the difference, you might pay top dollar for a potential show horse only to find you can't show him as a National Show Horse because his sire wasn't in the official registry. However, if the Arab half of the parents was registered, you could still show your horse as a half-Arab.

Other common crosses are almost anything crossed with Thoroughbreds; Quarter Horse x Appaloosas; and Quarter Horse x Paints.

Grade Horses

A term you may run into when looking at crossbred horses is *grade*. A grade horse is an unregistered horse of uncertain parentage. Even if you know the parentage, the horse technically is a grade horse if he doesn't have papers. He's comparable with a mutt dog: Some of the best dogs in the world are mutts, and some great horses are grade horses.

If you like the horse and he suits you, by all means consider him, whatever his pedigree. But if you plan to show, you'll be limited to "open" shows and classes. You won't be able to go to Quarter Horse shows, for example, even if you're sure your horse is one, because you won't have a registered Quarter Horse.

Ponies

More ill words are spoken about ponies than any other type of horse. Everybody has heard about ponies that bite, kick, scrape riders off on trees, and run away. The good stories about ponies don't get nearly the same publicity.

There are wonderful ponies out in the world that have carried children safely on trails, in horse shows, and in parades. It's not uncommon for good ponies to be passed, almost like heirlooms, to good new owners when a child outgrows his or her pony mount.

The main advantage of ponies is that they are not intimidating in size for small riders. There are a few breeds you might run into when looking for a pony, but often a good pony has a completely unknown pedigree. In other words, he's a grade pony.

Connemara

This breed originated in Ireland. Connemaras are medium to large in size; some are over 14.2h and are technically horses. These are sturdy animals that are often gray. They're known for their talent as jumpers. In this country, Connemaras are found in areas where people like to hunt and jump. There's no reason they can't be used for Western riding.

Hackney

Hackney ponies were bred to be high-stepping, fancy carriage ponies. In the show ring, they're prancing ponies that snap their knees almost up to their chins. They sometimes have docked tails. Hackneys are usually bay or dark brown with little white, sometimes have Roman noses, and sometimes truly plain heads. They're among the hottest of the pony breeds.

Hackneys are inclined to be feisty. Some that weren't born with the classic knee and hock action are sold at very reasonable prices.

With careful, consistent, and gentle handling these ponies can become very affectionate and reliable mounts for children. But be advised that if the children, or the trainer, are going to get into fights with their ponies, these ponies may fight right back. For this reason Hackneys should be trained by people with gentle consistency, not hot tempers. More than a few Hackneys are brilliant jumpers; others have been used for everything from pleasure driving to trail mounts, and even as small roping horses. These can be great ponies, but if they just retired from the Hackney show circuit, they may be too much for a new rider. (There are also Hackney horses. Quite rare in the United States, these horses are used primarily as carriage horses but can be ridden. They are slightly more common in Canada and stand up to 16h.)

Haflinger

Some fanciers refer to these stocky ponies as "the tractors of the Alps," which is an appropriate designation. The breed originated in Austria, where farmers needed horses for plowing and farmwork but didn't have big-enough farms or large-enough expanses of flat land to justify huge draft horses. Thus they developed a sturdy smaller breed that could do the plowing and also be driven or ridden briskly to town when the need arose.

Haflingers are always red or blond. They have long, thick, flaxen manes and tails, and almost always some sort of blaze on the face. They often have white socks or stockings. They're known for their rock-solid dispositions, and are seldom flighty or nervous.

A well-selected Haflinger is an excellent choice for a child's mount, unless he's too wide for the child to sit on. Haflingers are certainly up to carrying small to midsize adults.

The downside? Haflingers are not the most common breed around, and breeders of good animals keep their prices up. Also, these ponies occasionally function as equine tanks; a few have been known to bulldoze their way out of stalls and through fences.

Haflingers are probably most common in parts of the country where draft horses are still common. You're most likely to see them in draft harness in parades and shows, but they make fine riding horses, too, especially if you aren't interested in blazing speed.

Pony of the Americas (POA)

POAs, as they're called, are pony-size Appaloosas. Their colors are similar to Appaloosas. They're often seen in Western Pony classes and in contest events, although there's no reason they can't appear in English Pony classes. Like their Appaloosa cousins, many POAs are extremely athletic. As with Appaloosas, make sure you have the eyes checked before you buy.

Quarter Pony

A Quarter Pony is a Quarter Horse that didn't get quite big enough. The International Quarter Pony Association holds its own shows. Quarter Ponies are also often seen at 4-H shows in both the Western and the English riding divisions. They can make excellent mounts for children and small adults.

Shetland

Most people picture a Shetland as a small, fuzzy pony that demands carrots. Shetlands are a breed that originated in the Shetland Islands of Great Britain. They were small, stocky ponies used in the coal mines to pull loads.

In the United States, they're a popular type of pony for children. In the early 1970s, the Shetland Pony Association changed the type of pony it wanted to see in the show ring. Instead of the fuzzy backyard variety, show Shetlands became long-legged, long-necked, dark show ponies that look a great deal like Hackneys. But the backyard version continues to exist.

Consequently, there are now two types of Shetlands. The old-style Shetland is the stocky, fuzzy pony officially designated as the classic Shetland. The show Shetland is the high-stepping, hot show pony.

For a first mount for a child, you'll probably have more success with an old-style pony. Be aware that small ponies are sensitive to weight, and they quickly learn body language. They know instantly who knows how to ride and who doesn't, and they can be quick to take advantage of a situation.

Welsh

Welsh ponies originated, of course, in Wales. They're available in different sizes, ranging from about the size of the classic Shetlands to Welsh Cobs, which are horse size. In shows for Welsh ponies, the different sizes are designated and shown separately. The breed is reputed to have a good disposition. (Remember, though, that within any breed an individual can vary from the norm.)

Veterinarians say Welsh ponies have the best joints of any breed of horse or pony. This means they should hold up to work.

Welsh ponies are ridden by children and, as driving increases in popularity, are increasingly being driven by adults. Welsh ponies are often seen at hunter shows as children's mounts because they're usually quite attractive as well as good, reliable jumpers. They're less often seen at Western shows, although there's no good reason not to select a Welsh pony for Western riding.

Five-Gaited Horses, Amblers, and Pacers

Most horses have three gaits: the walk, the trot, and the canter. Since the canter is a slow version of the gallop, the gaits are occasionally called the walk, the trot, and the gallop. However, a small proportion of horses also pace, and some amble.

A variety of horse breeds have in fact been developed because of their ability to amble or pace. True pacers are used for racing, and are now found among only one breed, the Standardbred. These are the horses that pull sulkies at incredible speed. Fast-pacing Standardbreds can race the mile in about the time it takes a fast Thoroughbred to gallop the mile and an eighth. Oddly enough, racing Standardbreds get faster every year, while racing Thoroughbreds don't.

Amblers are horses that almost pace, but not quite, and are found among several breeds. In each breed, the gait has been exaggerated in a slightly different way. The timing and the look of the gait are as a result quite different in the various breeds; the gait is also known by a different name in each breed. From the point of view of gait analysis, however, these are all the same thing. It's easy to get into fights on this point with breed enthusiasts. A useful technique is to bank this information and skip the arguments.

The Pace and the Amble

The pace is a two-beat gait in which the legs on the same side hit together. The left hind and left front strike together, then the right hind and right front.

The amble is almost a pace but not quite. Giraffes and llamas are natural amblers. Each foot strikes the ground separately, but the timing of the footfalls is different than in the walk. If you hear a horse ambling, you usually hear an indistinct four-beat rhythm. Sometimes, the amble can be quite fast. The timing of the footfalls and the look of the amble are different in each breed in which the gait occurs, and it's given a different name in each breed.

American Saddle Horse (Saddlebreds)

This breed is best known for its brilliance in the show ring. American Saddle Horses, in fact, are almost always called the "peacocks of the show ring," an appropriate designation.

They're typically long-legged, high-headed horses of great elegance. Outside of horse shows, they aren't well known in much of the United States. Still, they're the horses of choice for pleasure riding where the breed is familiar.

Many people seem to think that because these animals are fiery in horse show classes, the breed is wild and unmanageable. This is simply not the case. In rural Missouri, Kentucky, and Tennessee, Saddlebreds (as they are also known) are widely used as pleasure, trail, and sometimes even ranch horses. They're spirited, but sensible.

Saddlebreds were developed in plantation days for gentlemen to ride comfortably. Even in this day, good Saddlebreds are wonderful riding horses. Of course this is a generalization, and not all individuals will fit the description, but Saddlebreds have a large and growing fan club, with good reason. If nice, sound Saddlebreds are available in your price range, don't be afraid to consider them. But if you hope to learn to compete in dressage one day, the high headedness typical of this breed may be a problem as you progress in your training.

Similarly, if you want to take up something like barrel racing or roping, you'll probably find that the long leggedness and high center of gravity characteristic of these horses make them less than suitable.

A confusing term you might run across when discussing Saddlebreds is *walk/trot horse,* which is a show term. Saddlebreds are either shown as five-gaited or three-gaited horses. The three-gaited type are known as walk/trot horses, even though they walk, trot, and canter. Three-gaited show horses usually have a *roached* mane: a mane that's clipped very short. Five-gaited Saddlebreds are shown with full manes.

A show Saddlebred that's a "pleasure horse" is one that's competed in a specific class: English Pleasure. These horses are very decidedly show horses, and may not be suitable for casual trail riding. A more appropriate Saddlebred for the newer rider is probably one that has competed in the class called Country Pleasure.

Saddlebred Gaits

Some terms you'll run across if you are talking about Saddlebreds in the show ring or on the trail include *rack, stepping pace, slow gait,* and *five gaited.*

Most horses that amble do so in place of trotting and have three gaits: the walk, the amble (whatever it happens to be called in that breed), and the canter. The American Saddle Horse, however, may walk, trot, and canter, but some also amble. The slow amble is called the *slow gait;* when it is fast it becomes the *rack.*

The rack used to be known as the stepping pace. It's a very smooth, fast gait. Show Saddlebreds that rack are trained to snap their knees and hocks so that the gait is quite spectacular to watch. Nonshow, pleasure horses that rack are less dramatic, but smooth. During the rack, the entire weight of the horse is at times borne by one leg. For this reason, the show rack is an especially tiring gait for the horse. The pleasure rack is much less demanding on the animal, because the suspension is not as pronounced or as long.

Icelandic Horses

These furry little animals are really ponies by American standards, but in the Icelandic tradition owners prefer to call them horses. It doesn't much matter which name you prefer. Icelandics can lay claim to the title as the oldest pure breed in the world. The first horses were shipped to Iceland with the Vikings in the ninth century, but in the year 930, by an act of the First Icelandic Parliament, further imports of horses into Iceland were banned. That law is still in effect today, so all the Icelandic horses in the world derive from the original Viking animals.

Over the thousand years since they got to Iceland, the breed has been developed to produce horses with a natural ambling gait known as the *tolt*, which is smooth and can be remarkably fast. Horses were also selected to have a breed characteristic of friendliness.

Icelandic horses have been exported to Europe for many years, and recently they have begun arriving and being bred in the United States. They're very suitable mounts for children and can carry bigger adults than you'd imagine, but probably aren't large enough for very large adults. They can be ridden or driven.

It's not surprising that Icelandics grow unbelievable hair coats, considering where they come from. That hair is cherished; it's never clipped off when the horses are shown. These little animals are making a name for themselves by doing some great group demonstrations at large horse expositions, usually leaving the crowds cheering at their speed and agility at the tolt. Icelandics are allowed to canter and gallop, although many can tolt nearly as fast.

Paso Horses

Pasos are amblers that originated in Puerto Rico, the Carribean, and Central and South America. Their history goes all the way back to the first shipment of horses to the New World by the Spanish, which included some amblers. By 1495, Columbus was importing breeding stock.

These first imports to our hemisphere had to be some of the toughest horses of all time. They were shipped across the ocean on the top deck of the ship, and were kept from moving around or washing overboard by being hung in slings with their feet just off the ground and their front feet tied together. They had no protection from wind, sun, or sea during months on the ocean. When the ships finally arrived near land, the horses were pushed overboard and had to swim to shore.

Not long after the first load of horses arrived in the New World, breeding farms were set up on islands throughout the Caribbean. From these came Pasos. They were developed a little differently at each location. Those that had to carry people over sand dunes were selected to have a peculiar winging gait, which was an adaptation for deep sand. If you watch one of these horses come toward you, you'll see him move each front leg forward and in a wide arc to the side with each step. Pasos that came from less sandy beginnings don't have this trait.

Amblers were popular then for the same reasons they are now: They're not only sturdy but also comfortable to ride, and they can go all day.

Pasos are inclined to be small horses with powerful, strongly arched necks. They often have long, thick manes and tails. Their gaits are the walk, a slow amble, and a fast amble. They aren't taught to canter.

Good Pasos are incredibly smooth to ride, and are capable of tremendous endurance and brisk speed. They're used for ranchwork in Central America and Puerto Rico. In the United States they usually serve as show horses, or as pleasure riding and trail horses.

If you ever have the chance to go to a Paso show, do so. One of the classes you'll find there is Most Classic Paso, in which the horses are judged on conformation and way of going. They're ridden one at a time down a raised wooden platform; as each one travels down, the judge requires him to halt and then move promptly forward. The raised platform serves as a sounding board for the horse's feet. The judge listens to the gait, and is very particular about how quickly the horse strikes the correct gait from the halt.

In the United States, Pasos are rare in many areas, and plentiful in a few hot spots. Florida and California probably have the most, but there are some in parts of the Midwest. Don't expect to find many giant-size Pasos; many are under 15h.

Pasos come in all solid colors, as well as roans, Palominos, and Pintos.

There are several breeds of Paso horses. The best known in the United States is the Paso Fino. From Peru comes the Peruvian Paso, which is a slightly larger and wider breed of ambling horse that was developed within the borders of Peru. While this breed shares Spanish ancestors with the Paso Fino, the stock from which it arose was imported by an entirely different group of settlers. As of this writing, Peruvian Pasos are found primarily in California, but expect to find them elsewhere soon!

Racking Horses, Fox Trotters, and Rocky Mountain Horses

In some parts of the country, especially Ohio, Kentucky, Tennessee, Missouri, and West Virginia, is a breed called the Racking Horse. These horses may have mixed ancestry that usually includes Tennessee Walker. They're used as pleasure and trail animals, and there are horse shows just for them.

Racking races are often held for these horses, or classes in which the speed of the rack counts for almost everything. Racking horses may not snap their knees and hocks as much as show Saddlebreds, but they can fly at the rack.

The Racking Horse Association recently decided to make its horses into a true breed and thus requires pedigrees; it no longer registers just any horse that racks. As time goes on, the registry is likely to become even more restrictive, requiring new foals to be offspring only of registered parents.

From rural Missouri comes the Missouri Fox Trotter. Its gait is a smooth amble that isn't extremely exaggerated. These horses are used for trail and pleasure riding, and also have their own shows. They look something like Quarter Horses that amble and are rarely found outside the south-central states, although some western parks are importing them for trail horses and crossing them with donkeys to get smooth-gaited riding mules.

Probably the rarest of all the ambling breeds is the Rocky Mountain Horse. Interestingly, you aren't likely to find one in the Rocky Mountains, although that's where the foundation sire of the breed earned his reputation.

These are small, sturdy horses with quiet dispositions, often found in Kentucky and southern Ohio. The Rocky Mountain Horse Association is tiny but active in promoting the breed. If you contact the association, it will help you find a Rocky Mountain Horse to try. Like the other ambling breeds, these horses are great for pleasure and trail riding, but not ideal if you plan to jump or do contest riding.

Standardbred

Standardbreds were developed as racehorses. The name *Standardbred* comes from the tradition of requiring the horses to trot or pace to a timed standard. If a horse wasn't fast enough, he wasn't allowed in the registry.

Standardbreds, as mentioned before, are used in driving races. They're also the most common Amish buggy horses. Many are true pacers, but there are also bloodlines that produce natural trotters. These compete in trotting races, but trotters and pacers are never raced against each other. Pacing Standardbreds are, on average, a little faster than their trotting kin.

Up until the 1920s and 1930s, there were races for pacers and trotters under saddle. The tradition nearly became extinct, but seems to be making a bit of a comeback of late.

Some people allege that pacers are uncomfortable to ride, although in Colonial times and before it was common to ride them, and they were sought after. There's really no good reason not to ride them.

Standardbreds are usually small to medium-size horses of dark color. There are a few grays in the breed and a smattering of chestnuts and roans, but most tend to be bay, brown, or black, without much white. Standardbred enthusiasts dislike light-colored horses. This preference goes back to the days before dry cleaners: Most Colonial people wore black wool coats, which looked awful when covered with white horsehair. So the ever-practical farmer/horse breeders selected dark-colored horses. To this day, the Amish prefer dark driving horses for the same reason.

Standardbreds have thick manes and tails. More than a few have plain heads. Although the breed isn't well suited for jumping or galloping sports like barrel racing, these horses are incredibly tough and capable of tremendous endurance. They're common in states where they're raced, but nearly unknown in other parts of the United States.

In areas where this breed is common, you may easily find a suitable mount at a good price. If you're interested in endurance or trail riding, and there are Standardbreds in your area, you might want to look at one. If you're thinking about taking up pleasure driving you should definitely look at Standardbreds. Horses that are past their racing prime, if they pass a veterinarian's check, can have a long and useful life as driving or riding horses. Almost all horses that paced on the racetrack are happy to trot when they don't have to go at race speed, in race equipment.

Retired Standardbreds

One great advantage of owning a retired racing Standardbred is that these horses are used to lots of work, and they've been driven close to tractors, cars, crowds of people, and nearly everything else, so they aren't inclined to shy.

There are organizations that try to place retired racing Standardbreds in pleasure homes, and there's now an association for showing Standardbreds that includes many Under-Saddle classes. Wise police departments often retrain retired Standardbreds to make useful police horses as well.

Tennessee Walker

Tennessee Walking Horses are ambling horses developed by plantation owners in the southern colonies of early America to ride for hours as they surveyed their estates. They were said to be especially useful when riding through narrow crop rows.

Walkers walk and canter just like any other horse breed, but instead of trotting, they Tennessee walk. This is an amble exaggerated in such a way that the hind legs of the horse take long, nearly shuffling steps. Each hind leg comes well up beneath the body of the horse on each step. The front feet reach out far in front of the horse.

Tennessee Walkers used for show were once subjected to cruel training methods: They were lamed in both front legs so they'd have to carry more weight and take larger steps with their hind legs. Thankfully, public outcry has gone a long way toward stopping this practice.

The breed is considered steady and even tempered, and has an incredibly smooth gait. In the running walk, a Tennessee Walker can move as fast as another horse might canter. Some are large, but they're usually gentle. Outside the show world, Walkers are widely used as trail horses.

Walking Horses come in all solid colors as well as roans. True black horses are quite common in the breed.

4

Accommodations for Your Horse

If you're purchasing a horse, it's important to decide where she's going to live and to make all the appropriate arrangements *before* the trailer arrives to deliver her. Basically, you have two options: You can board your horse at a stable, or, if you have sufficient acres of "horse" land, you may be able to keep her at home.

In general, if you have limited horse-care knowledge, you're probably better off stabling your horse initially. Then, as you acquire horse-care expertise through exposure to a well-run barn, you can consider bringing your horse home and caring for her yourself.

While your horse is stabled, you can learn how to muck a stall properly (you'll need a strong back), feed her, and water her. With a good mentor, you can learn a lot about animal husbandry, too. If you're thinking of keeping your horse at home, it would be a good idea to try out the physical aspects of horse care — take a week's vacation and work as a stable hand. You'll quickly learn the amount of time and physical strength needed to care for a horse on a daily basis.

Of course, the decision whether to board your horse or keep her at home really depends on many factors, including what kind of experiences you want from owning a horse, your financial situation, your current lifestyle and career demands, and, of course, whether your property is suitable and zoned for horses.

Both stabling and keeping a horse at home can be tremendously positive experiences; however, the same high-quality facilities (barn or shelter, fencing, pastures, and so on) that are necessary for a good stable experience are also critical to keeping a horse at home. If you're sitting on the fence on this issue, consider the pros and cons of each option.

The Advantages of Stabling

Boarding your horse at a full-service facility has several advantages. For starters, a stable provides "carefree" horse ownership. All or most stable chores — mucking, mowing, feeding, watering, turnout, and so on — are taken care of for you. This means you'll have much more time for riding.

Additionally, a full-service barn may make your life a little less stressful; if you're trying to meet a deadline at work, for instance, you don't have to worry about rushing home to make sure your horse is fed. Similarly, if you want to take a two-week vacation to the Bahamas, you can go without having to make any complex arrangements for horse care.

A good stable will offer a variety of facilities for your riding enjoyment. A hunter/jumper stable may have multiple riding rings with and without jumps, and perhaps an outdoor course. A Western barn as well as some English barns may offer its boarders access to trails and open pastures for weekend rides. A real plus is an indoor riding arena that can be used during inclement weather or at night. Many stables have trailers or vans to take boarders to horse shows or trailheads, too.

Stables typically offer other services as well, such as riding instruction, training (your horse may need a little work beyond your current skill level), and exercise on days you can't ride. There may be someone willing to clean and care for your tack.

At a well-run barn, the staff sees to most of your horse's needs.
▼

Another big draw to a stable is the fact that your horse receives near-constant supervision. In a barn with a full-time manager, there's usually someone around and something going on. If your horse becomes ill or injures herself, it will be noticed relatively quickly; the experienced manager will understand the severity of the situation, take appropriate action, and notify you.

And finally, don't forget the social aspect of riding. If you enjoy being around other people with like interests (horses), it's fun to ride at an active stable.

The Disadvantages of Stabling

When you board at a large or very active stable, you seldom have the arena to yourself. You may be competing for use of the facility with riding students and other boarders; you may also be in competition for cross-ties and lead ropes. Your carrot supply might constantly dwindle and your grooming supplies get more use than you are giving them, unless you have a tack trunk with a lock. If the stable manager doesn't run a tight ship and keep a close rein on boarders, you may not be able to take advantage of all the stable's great facilities.

Which brings up another potential downside to boarding at a stable. Good management can be hard to find — but it can be even harder to keep. Many stables have difficulty keeping good managers for any period of time. So you may bring your horse to a terrific stable only to have the manager leave in a month and be replaced by someone only mediocre. The same is true for trainers. If the stable isn't owned by a trainer, or if the trainer doesn't own an interest in the stables, he or she could be gone overnight.

The Advantages of Home Horsekeeping

One of the greatest joys of owning a horse and keeping her at home is that you can ride anytime you feel like it. You don't have to commute to the stable each day; walk out your back door and down to the barn, and you're ready to go.

With home horsekeeping, you don't have to rely on others for your horse care. You are the provider (unless you opt to pay someone to do the stable chores) and are in sole control of the level of care your horse receives. In other words, you can make sure your horse receives the ultimate in care.

▶ *These horses have plenty of room for grazing and socializing.*

Another advantage to boarding your horse at home can be lower monthly expenses than if you boarded her at a stable — if, that is, you already live on property that has a suitable barn or shelter, pastures, and an area to ride.

The Disadvantages of Home Horsekeeping

Preparing your property for horse ownership can be a major endeavor, especially if you have to build a barn or shelter, clear trees for a pasture, and install fencing. If you're going to be the person responsible for mucking, feeding, watering, turning out your horse, and maintaining fences, you may find you have less time for riding than you expected. If you're limited to a one-hour time slot after work each day to ride, you may find yourself in a serious time crunch.

Also, how strong are you? The physical fitness required to ride a horse or many horses each day is quite different from the strength required to stack 50-pound bales of hay, carry grain bags from the truck to the barn, and pitchfork heavy, wet bedding into a wheelbarrow. Even if you think these physical chores will pose no problem, be sure you try them for several days in a row first. And remember, these tasks must be done in all kinds of weather.

Another point to consider before you bring your new horse home is how social you are. If you'd really enjoy being around other riders, boarding your horse at home may become quite lonely unless more than one person in your family rides, or you have neighbors whom you enjoy and who like to ride.

Are you a beginning rider? Or someone who wants to continue honing horsemanship skills? If you're serious about competing, you'll most likely want to take riding lessons. If you board your horse at home, either you'll need to pay a trainer to come out to your home to give you lessons, or you'll need to trailer your horse to a facility at which a trainer will give "outsiders" lessons.

Home horsekeeping is a 24-hour-a-day, 7-day-a-week responsibility. If you want to go on vacation, you'll have to find someone reliable (a key word here) whom you can pay to care for your horse while you're gone.

Perhaps most important: Realize that when keeping your horse at home, the health and safety of your horse is your responsibility. Will you be home enough to notice the early signs of a problem? Will you recognize subtle signs of illness?

Ultimately, the decision lies with you and what will work out best for your situation. Regardless of where you decide to keep your horse, you'll need to make sure her accommodations are safe and meet her many needs. Remember that the basic

To keep your horse at home, you need to be able to do the work it requires — or hire someone to do it for you.
▼

requirements you'd look for when selecting a stable (stall measurements, types of bedding, pasture care, fencing, and so on) are the same ones you'll need to provide your horse if you keep her at home. (See Recommended Reading for more information on backyard or home horsekeeping.)

The Stable

If you've been taking lessons at a local stable and are buying your horse through the manager or a trainer there, the most sensible option for you is probably to board your horse at this same stable. You're familiar and comfortable with the barn, and when you change roles from "lesson rider" to "horse owner," the transition should be a smooth and enjoyable one.

If, however, you're not currently affiliated with a barn, nor are you buying your horse from a stable at which you'd like to board her (perhaps it's too far away), you need to learn what to look for in a stable. Even if you're planning to board your horse at home, you may still need to search out a good stable at which to board her until your horse shelter and grounds are ready for her to move in.

Be sure to visit several barns in your area so that you can make good comparisons and a well-researched decision. When you go to check each one out, the first thing you should do is form a general impression; then look for details. Your first clues to a well-run barn are the condition of the horses and the pride that's taken in maintaining a clean and efficient barn. When you're given a tour of the facility, take a look at the horses. Are they well fed? Are their coats glossy and well groomed? Are they calm yet attentive when you pass by, or dull and sluggish?

When you speak to the manager, does he or she give the impression of being knowledgeable and trustworthy? Since this is the person who runs the whole operation, he or she should be someone you can trust implicitly with your horse, who welcomes questions, and with whom you can discuss any concerns freely.

Another general situation to be aware of is the type of riding most people do at a prospective barn and how it compares with yours. If everybody at the barn rides Western and you want to jump, for example, you may find that the other boarders don't appreciate your setting up fences all

---

Referrals

If you're a boarder in search of a barn, narrow your search by asking questions. Ask the person from whom you're buying your horse if he or she can recommend a stable in your area. Ask your veterinarian the same question. Query the owner of the local feed store. Talk to horse owners in your area. If you ask enough people, you'll find the same stable names coming up again and again as highly recommended — and probably a few that should be avoided.

over the arena — or there may be no facilities for you to practice jumping at all. If you enjoy driving your horse, make sure there are areas where you can do this and a storage area in which to keep your equipment. Trail riders obviously need to make sure there are trails.

You should also consider your own reaction to the people at the barn. Your horse is supposed to be your recreation; if you don't get along with the people at the barn, you may find yourself riding alone a lot, or wishing you could. Riders often enjoy their horses more if they like the people who share the sport with them. If you don't care much about other riders and tend to do your own thing, then the other boarders shouldn't be a factor.

Ultimately, of course, the care of the horse is your primary concern, and a quality stable with a few unfriendly riders should be higher on your list than a barn with friendly riders and substandard conditions for horses. Again, consider your needs and resources. If you have sufficient acreage, an adequate shelter, and the time you need to care for your horse at home, this might be the best option for you and for her.

▲

For many first-time horse buyers, locating a good stable or barn is an important first step. Start looking for one early in the process, before *you buy your horse.*

▲

Home horsekeeping is an attractive option for many — just be sure you have adequate acreage to support your horse's needs, and provide sufficient shelter, fencing, and water, too. This shelter is an economical alternative to a barn.

What to Look for in a Stable or Barn

When you're considering a stable or barn, form a general impression first. If it's favorable, then consider whether the facility is suited for your particular needs:

✓ Are the horses well fed?

✓ Are the horses' coats glossy and well groomed?

✓ Are the horses calm yet attentive when you pass by?

✓ Does the manager seem knowledgeable and trustworthy?

✓ What type of riding is most common?

✓ Do the other riders seem friendly?

✓ Are the facilities well maintained, safe, and adequate for your needs?

✓ What services are offered?

Pasturing

For riders not inclined to show and who simply want their horse for pleasure riding, she may do very well if left out in a pasture all year with a three-sided, roofed shelter (its back side positioned against the prevailing winds, which usually are from the north or west). This is an economical option for owners who want to keep their horses at home but can't afford to build a barn. Healthy horses will do quite well — even in the snow — if they have sufficient shelter. As long as your horse can stay dry in her shelter during a cold rain, she should be fine. You'll need to provide a watering trough (an automatic waterer makes the job of keeping this full much easier), and you'll also need to keep the shelter area picked up and clean. Adequate fencing is also a must. (See Recommended Reading for more ideas on home horsekeeping.)

Fire Safety

If you choose to board your horse or even if you decide to keep her at home, fire hazards are always a concern simply because so many things in a barn or shelter are flammable. There are wooden stalls and hay, and most bedding materials can catch fire quickly. For this reason, smoking should not be tolerated at a barn or near a shelter.

At a barn or stable, NO SMOKING signs should be prominently posted and enforced. Under no conditions should boarders or stable hands be allowed to smoke in any area in or around the barn — particularly anywhere hay is stored. Fire extinguishers should be readily available and mounted in areas that are easy to see and reach.

Electrical wiring is another, less obvious fire hazard. Any wires that pass near stalls should be encased in a conduit to keep horses from biting them. Electrical switches should be well maintained and shouldn't spark or crackle when turned on and off. Cobwebs should be kept to a minimum, too: They are a significant fire hazard.

The Stall

Whether you're keeping your horse at home or boarding her at a stable, she should have her own stall unless you plan to field-board her with an adequate outdoor shelter.

The stall should be clean, dry, well ventilated, and bright, with a good level floor and no obvious places (such as a sharp corner on a hay rack, or a bit of wire tying something together) for your horse to get hurt. It should be constructed of heavy, solid, thick wooden boards. The minimum size for a stall for a full-size horse is 10 feet by 12 feet; larger, if you have a larger horse. A 10-foot by 10-foot stall may be suitable for a pony but not a horse. Generally, in a properly sized stall, the horse will be able to turn around comfortably and to lie down easily.

▲
This stall is large, safe, and comfortable.

Ventilation and Light

Ventilation in a barn is important in both summer and winter months. In the summer, a barn should be open and breezy. Horses are absolutely miserable in hot, stuffy quarters.

Large stables can provide good ventilation in a variety of ways. If you ever see the grand horse barns of Kentucky's Thoroughbred farms, you'll note that many have cupolas. Besides looking nice, a cupola also serves as an area to which hot air can rise and be pulled out through fans or vents that can be opened in summer months. Other barns may have almost cathedral-like ceilings, usually surrounded by windows to allow in lots of sunlight and plenty of ventilation. Some barns may simply have an industrial fan located at one end of the roof to draw hot air out in the summer. The best-ventilated barns have no overhead hay storage.

Ventilation during the winter is important, too. A cold, well-ventilated barn may not be very comfortable for you, but it's truly healthier for your horse. Horses are built for winter; they have fewer respiratory problems in barns with circulating air than in barns that are very snug and warm.

Part and parcel of good ventilation is the presence of windows, which not only give the barn owner the ability to open the place up in hot months and allow more air circulation, but also provide horses and owners with much natural light during both summer and winter months.

Windows also give horses the opportunity to watch what's going on. Some stalls are designed so that in pleasant months, horses can look out both into the barn (through bars into a center aisle) and outside (perhaps through the top of a Dutch door or large window). Horses get bored in their stalls just as you would, so a "room with a view" is a nice way to keep them entertained. A horse should never live in a dark, closed-in box!

If you have the job of designing a barn for your horse at home, it's a good idea to visit some area stables to get ideas about what configurations work and what don't. You'll also need to give some thought to the placement of the barn on your property to take full advantage of any summer breezes you have. (See Recommended Reading for some valuable books on building barns. They'll give you invaluable insight into how to build a barn that is bright year-round yet cool in the summer and tight in the winter.)

Floor

Uneven stall floors are hard on a horse's legs, and they also tend to gather wet pools and damp spots. For these reasons, the floor of the stall should be relatively smooth and constructed of materials suitable for horses.

If you're building your own barn or shelter, installing a horse-friendly floor is essential. If you choose to board your horse, be sure to check a few stalls in the prospective barn or stable carefully to ensure that the flooring passes muster.

Flooring Materials

One common, well-liked type of floor is made of either dirt or packed clay. Dirt and clay floors provide good cushioning for a horse's legs. Adequate cushioning is especially critical if your horse is active in performance events, if she is getting on in years, or if she simply has sensitive legs. Because dirt and clay are soft, as well as for the safety of your horse, floors made of these materials must be maintained regularly. How often depends on drainage and the stall's occupant. Clay drains poorly, so with a clay floor, odor may be a major problem. (Chemicals are available that will almost eliminate bad odors, however.) If your horse paws a hole in the floor of her stall, it must be filled immediately to prevent possible injuries.

A mix of dirt or clay and very fine limestone dust that's packed tightly is another flooring option. This type of flooring drains well. It provides a harder base than dirt or packed clay, but if enough bedding is provided the amount of cushioning will be fine for most horses.

Because of its wide availability, concrete may be a tempting flooring option — and it's fairly common in rebuilt dairy barns — but it's not the best surface for horses and generally should be avoided, if possible. Some owners find that concrete is too hard for their horses, even if it's well bedded or covered with rubber stall mats (a combination of rubber, nylon, and rayon). A horse boarded in a stall with a concrete floor may develop swollen legs or appear to be stiff and sore. Still, some horsemen prefer a well-bedded concrete floor, because it stays level (unlike a dirt floor).

Wood floors are common in older barns. If a stall with wood floors is not well bedded, the horse can get abrasions and possibly even splinters from getting up and down. Odor can also be a problem with wood floors, but chemicals can help tremendously to eliminate it. A well-bedded wood floor is a perfectly acceptable option.

Bedding

Stalls may be bedded with any of several materials. The most common are straw and wood shavings or sawdust. Straw can provide good soft, warm bedding, if it's deep enough. Urine tends to soak to the bottom, so the top stays relatively dry.

The disadvantage of straw is that some horses may eat it. Depending on the horse's appetite, straw may incline her to colic. If you're planning a barn at home, keep in mind that mucking a stall with straw bedding can make for a large manure pile (you'll go through a lot), and in some areas of the country using straw for bedding can be expensive. As well, a stall with straw bedding takes about twice as long to muck as one with shavings.

Wood shavings, especially pine shavings, can make very nice bedding for horses. The pine types, which may or may not be expensive in your area of the United States, are absorbent and soft, and help control odor. The type of wood shavings available in your area may vary, but if pine shavings are affordable, most types are good bets for stall bedding.

Sawdust can be an inexpensive bedding option, and it's quite absorbent. Since horses can breathe in the little bits of dust very easily, however, it shouldn't be used if your horse is prone to respiratory problems, or if you don't have a source for dry sawdust.

Depending on your area, you may also find other regional types of bedding. For example, in the South, peanut hulls are often used as winter bedding at large horse farms. Hulls are absorbent, and they're inexpensive in that area. They're only used in the winter, however, because they attract too many flies in the summer. Another bedding material you find in some southern areas is grass. This is said to be quite good.

Whatever bedding is used by the barn you examine, it should be deep enough to form a good cushion, and the stalls should be clean and dry. This "clean-and-dry" aspect relies heavily on the determination, experience, and work ethic of the hired help.

Stall mucking is labor intensive; wet bedding is *heavy*, and even a small horse that drinks a lot can produce a very wet stall. So if a stable hand has any tendency toward laziness, it'll show up in the stalls. Or if the management is trying to cut corners to beat costs, you may find too little bedding in the horses' stalls. Neither situation is good.

If you're keeping your horse at home, make sure you do this job right, too! The stall should be bedded deeply enough that the horse has a nice cushion to lie on. The stall should also be kept dry and free of intense ammonia odor. A wet, urine-soaked stall not only smells bad, but it's also bad for your horse's hooves; it can cause thrush and a whole host of other problems. If you're pasturing your horse, keep her shelter area picked up on a regular basis and provide some bedding materials in cold months.

Black Walnut Warning!

Black walnut sawdust should *never* be used as horse bedding. Some horses have been shown to have a reaction to the wood from the black walnut tree. If your horse has such a sensitivity, she'll become sore in her legs or even founder when exposed to the wood for even a short amount of time. Be aware of this potential problem when securing bedding for your horse's stall. To prevent injury, discuss the issue with both the manager of the barn and your veterinarian.

Walls

Stall walls are generally around 8 feet tall; the wall facing the aisle is usually a partial wall, with bars, pipe, or mesh making up its top portion. The facing wall also contains a stall door, which may be hinged, sliding, or a combination of the two. The ceiling height for the stalls should be 12 feet, or at least high enough that your horse will not injure herself if she happens to rear.

Stall walls should be solidly constructed and well maintained, with no gaps a foot or leg could fit through. Walls should be made of oak, so that a kicking horse will not be able to put her foot through the wall. Sheet metal must never be used as a part of any stall wall, because horses can kick through it. If you're looking at boarding barns, make sure the walls of the stalls extend deeply into the floor. Any gaps at ground level can be catastrophic, because a horse can easily trap her foot.

The boards in the stalls should also be very smooth and contain no rough edges, protruding nails, or sharp bits of wire. If there's a sharp object in the stall, you can almost guarantee that your horse will find it and cut herself immediately. Your job is to make sure she doesn't have this opportunity. It's also important to make sure that no boards are cracked or loose.

The stall front should have a solid bottom half to avoid injury to the horse. The top half should be either open (such as a Dutch door) or constructed with bars or mesh, to prevent the stall occupant from nipping at passersby or attempting to make a break for freedom. In the former case, make sure your horse can't reach around and open the stall latch: Some horses are true escape artists. If the top of the stall front is made of bars, these should be strong and spaced closely enough together that your horse can't stick her muzzle or a foot through. If the top is of wire mesh, watch out for snags and bits of wire that poke into the stall.

Waterers and Feeders

Your horse should have access to clean water at all times. Horses drink 10 to 20 gallons a day. To meet your horse's water needs, the stall should have a space along the front wall for two buckets, which you may have to provide, or it should have a clean automatic waterer in it. One bucket is not enough unless it's checked every few hours like clockwork. Also, a bored or playful horse may tip her buckets when they're half full, so an additional hook may be needed to keep the water where it belongs.

In cold weather, thick layers of ice may form on the water buckets; these need to be routinely broken to allow the horse to drink adequately. If you're keeping your horse at home, you'll need to make sure the ice is broken frequently, too. It may be worthwhile to buy an insulated bucket. I don't recommend water heaters, which might pose a fire hazard.

The water buckets should be emptied and cleaned every morning. Horses aren't neat eaters — they're forever dropping food into water buckets. If the buckets aren't cleaned, the water becomes foul and the horses won't drink. Buckets are often black so it's sometimes hard to see the water's true color. Don't take a chance: Change the water and scrub the buckets often.

The stall should also have a feeder for grain, or a place for you to provide one. Make sure that the feeders are not placed on adjoining stall walls. If two horses are eating on the same dividing wall, they may repeatedly kick it. *(Hey, I can hear that horse over there. She's gonna eat my food!)*

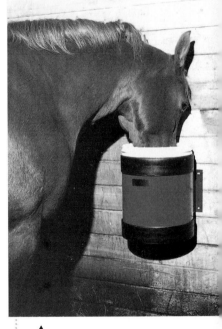

▲
An insulated water bucket is one way to help prevent water from freezing in winter. (Courtesy of Country Manufacturing.)

Also, check any hay racks in the stall. Hay can be fed to horses on the floor, or elevated on the stall wall in a synthetic mesh rope sack or a hay rack made of metal bars. If the stall does have such a hay rack, make sure there aren't any sharp corners your horse could hit her head on, or places to get a foot caught if she's bouncing around the stall.

Worming and Vaccination Policies

In addition to making sure you like and trust your horse's veterinarian, be sure to ask a stable's management what its worming and vaccination policies are. A good barn will require all residents to be vaccinated for a variety of problems, and will require that they be wormed on a regular basis.

Boarding Costs

A good stable costs money. Great services and facilities certainly aren't free! Costs for boarding in metropolitan suburbs are moderate to high. If you select a barn farther away from an urban area, the cost is usually less.

A full-board, or full-service, barn usually meets most of your horse's needs. The barn cleans the stall, turns the horse out, feeds and waters her, and blankets her as necessary in the winter. All the chores required to maintain the property are covered by your monthly fee. You're generally responsible for grooming and exercising your horse, however.

At some barns, additional services such as worming and blanketing are included in the monthly board fee; some barns charge extra for these services.

A well-run barn is typically in great demand, so don't be surprised if there's a waiting list to obtain a place for your horse. You may have to wait until a boarder moves out. Always check out nearby barns and their availability *before* you buy your horse.

Do take into account the distance between your prospective stable and your home or job when considering overall cost. The barn you like may be higher priced, but if it saves you lots of driving time, it might be worth it. Remember, too, that you're buying a horse because you enjoy horses and riding. If a barn is too far from your home or work, boarding your horse there could discourage you from riding.

Under no circumstances should you settle for a stable that will possibly subject your horse to ill treatment or danger. Take your time and keep looking until you find the stable that offers the best balance of good horse care, facilities that suit your riding needs, and price.

Costs of Boarding at Home

If you keep your horse at home, your monthly expenses will likely be significantly lower than they would be if you boarded her at a full-service barn. The costs to you in time and effort, on the other hand, will be significantly higher. If your schedule is flexible and you welcome what at times can be the challenging task of keeping your horse well cared for, you'll probably be very happy to have her at home.

Keep in mind that at a boarding barn, barn staff get the hay and the grain, arrange for farrier and veterinary appointments, and do all maintenance and mowing, among other things. At home, all those chores are up to you. Even if you can afford the dollars, ask yourself whether you can afford the time.

Public Barn Areas

The public areas of a barn are the aisles, arenas, grooming areas, and tack rooms. If you're shopping for a stable, check out these areas to make sure they're safe and workable.

If you're considering constructing a barn on your own property, many different configurations are possible; your final choice of amenities will rest on balancing what you need, what you want, and, ultimately, what you can afford.

In general, the aisles of a barn, no matter what its size, should be kept free of objects that horses can get hung up on and hurt themselves. This includes rakes, wheelbarrows, ropes, boards, trash cans, and farm equipment, like manure spreaders. You don't want to have to try to squeeze your horse past a tractor and a harrow every time you go in and out.

The wash area for your horse should be free of any dangers, too.

Is This Stable Suitable?

To determine whether a prospective stable is suitable — for your horse and also for you — ask yourself these questions. Based on your answers, decide whether the facilities and services offered match your needs:

✓ Is the grain stored in such a way that a loose horse can't get to it?

✓ Do the riding areas look reasonably well maintained?

✓ Do the barn's operating hours suit your schedule?

✓ Is there a lighted outdoor arena where you can ride at night?

✓ Is there an indoor arena for riding in inclement weather?

✓ Will you have reasonable access to the riding areas?

✓ Is there a lesson program that will limit your arena access?

✓ Is there a place that you can lock where you can keep your saddle and bridle?

▲
The tack room should be neat and well kept.

The Tack Room

As you're checking out a stable, look at the tack room facilities. Do boarders keep their tack and grooming supplies in a community tack room? Or are these supplies kept on the stall fronts?

Generally, tack kept in a separate room remains cleaner (less dust from the aisle). It also may be less vulnerable to theft — if the tack room is locked every night. Your saddle, bridle(s), and riding equipment are quite costly and not items that you'd ever want stolen. Ask the management if there has ever been a problem with theft, and what measures are taken to prevent it.

You'll also want to make sure your saddle is covered by your own homeowner's insurance. Most barns' insurance will not cover you for your loss. Many boarders, even at the best barns, take their saddles home with them, just to be safe.

To discourage other boarders from borrowing and, ultimately, misplacing your equipment, write your name with indelible ink on virtually everything you own. (Items labeled like this are much more embarrassing to borrow!)

Liability Insurance

Even if you're boarding your horse at a private or public stable, make sure you have liability insurance. (Some barns require boarders to purchase this insurance.) Horses are unpredictable and even the quietest, most good-natured horse may find occasion to bite, kick, or otherwise hurt someone. Make sure you're protected against any potential lawsuits. Ask your homeowner's insurance agent, and see page 115 for more information.

Arenas and Other Riding Areas

Okay, you've looked closely at the stalls and visited the public areas of the barn and everything checks out pretty well. Now, where are you going to ride? If you're interested in trail riding, make sure you have access to safe, well-maintained trails. If you're more interested in showing your horse, you'll most likely want more facilities. Ideally, you should have at least one large outdoor ring and access to a lighted indoor arena. Both should be frequently raked smooth and have relatively deep, soft footing. If you're into jumping, it would be nice to have access to an outdoor course.

Access to Facilities

Once you've determined that a stable has the facilities you're looking for, make sure you'll be able to use them. When you talk to the manager, find out what the stable's hours are. Do they fit with your work schedule?

This indoor arena provides plenty of room for riders in inclement weather.

Also find out what time lessons are offered, and where boarders are required to ride during lesson time.

A common complaint among boarders is that lesson riders take priority, while boarders are treated like second-class citizens. Most stables don't allow boarders to ride in the same ring or arena as someone receiving a private or group lesson. That's okay if the alternate ring or arena meets your standards — or if you're never around to ride when the stable holds its lessons. However, if your riding hours continually conflict with lesson hours and you find yourself relegated to a small ring in which you and other boarders are virtually falling over each other, you might consider another stable that better meets your needs.

If you're planning to keep you horse at home, you'll never have a problem with conflicting schedules. However, you should carefully plan how to use your land to its best advantage — where to place pastures, outdoor rings, an arena, and so on. If you're serious about showing your horse and have room for only one ring, you might consider an indoor arena. Costly? Yes, extremely. However, you'll be able to ride in all types of weather and at night; your arena can also be opened up at either end to make an enjoyable "shaded" summer facility.

Pastures and Paddocks

At some stables, the only "pasture" available to boarders is an unused riding ring in which your horse can jump around and stretch her legs once a day. At other stables, your horse may be able to actually roam around in a large pasture with a few equine buddies and munch grass. Well-manicured pastures are, of course, the nicest option — but at a minimum, your horse should be given the opportunity for a daily "turnout."

When selecting a stable, be sure to ask the management about its turnout policies. Horses must be exercised. Ideally, your horse would spend her days roaming a large pasture, romping and playing at will until you arrive to ride her. If this isn't the arrangement at the stable, make sure your horse will receive some turnout time each day, regardless of whether you come to ride.

Some stables will only turn out horses if the owner hasn't shown up in several days and the horse is restless. This isn't good. You want a stable that will turn out horses on a routine basis or one that will honor your request to do so. Be advised that some barns may charge for this service. Make sure you ask and are comfortable with the barn's policies, and remember — horses must be exercised!

Another question to pose to the manager of a barn is how horses are turned out. In other words, how many horses are turned out at the same time, and how will the manager make sure your horse is not injured by the others?

Ideally, horses are divided by gender. Mares go out with mares, and geldings with geldings. There are many farms where geldings go out with a bunch of mares and everybody gets along just fine, but the introduction of a new horse can upset the social standing enough for several of the horses to get hurt. A new horse that's thrown out with an established herd may get picked on, which means bites, kicks, and being chased. Any introductions should be slow, well thought out, supervised, and in daylight.

Additionally, turnout numbers should be limited. If the barn has a small paddock, only one or two horses should be turned out together. A larger field can accommodate more horses, but with large groups of horses turned out together there are inevitably some scrapes and bruises; serious injury also sometimes occurs. Whatever the situation, the barn management should have a sensible plan for introducing your horse to the group.

If you're planning to keep your horse at home, the social problems of turnouts won't be yours to worry about; still, you'll need to make plans so that your horse can be turned out every day. In order to do this, you'll need to design your property to hold more than one pasture; otherwise, your

Turnout is good for horses. Look for stables that offer the following:

✓ Pastures for turnout

✓ Daily turnout

✓ Few horses in turnout at one time

✓ Horses grouped by gender in turnout to minimize fighting

✓ Staff to check on horses

✓ Safe, secure, well-maintained fencing

✓ Strong, safe gates that are easy to operate

✓ A constant supply of available water during turnout

▶ *Turnout is good for horses, so try to find a stable that has plenty of pasture and daily turnout.*

horse will overgraze and your lush pasture will eventually turn to trampled mud. Likewise, you'll need the equipment to mow a large pasture to keep the vegetation from overgrowing. And you'll need to carefully monitor the types of plants growing in your pastures. Some species are poisonous to horses, including milkweed, locoweed, yew, and buttercups. Be sure to check with your local Agricultural Extension Agent to find out what grows in your area, how to recognize it, and how to rid your pastures of it.

Fences

Good solid fencing in pastures and outdoor rings is essential to the health and welfare of your horse. If you're considering keeping your horse at home, make sure you budget for a quality fence and its upkeep.

Wooden Fencing

An excellent type of fencing is the aesthetically pleasing wooden-board fence. If properly built (posts on the outside and boards on the inside, to prevent boards from popping off if horses lean on the fence), this fencing provides you with a safe means to control your horse. The best is fencing designed with no corners at right angles to the pasture. Why? If more than one horse is running in the pasture, a curved corner prevents the animals from getting boxed in there.

The major downside to wooden fencing is the upkeep. If you're choosing a stable, take a look at how well maintained the fences are. Are there rusted nails protruding from the boards? Are there broken boards that haven't been replaced? Are the fences well painted or stained, or are they long overdue for a fresh coat?

◄
Wooden fencing is considered by many to be the most aesthetically pleasing of fencing choices.

If you're horsekeeping at home, wood fence is expensive to install, and fence boards need to be painted or stained on a regular basis to prevent weathering. Also, make sure you don't use pressure-treated wood in your fences. This type of wood has salts in it that are quite tasty to horses, as well as chemicals that may be toxic to them. If you have a pasture constructed with pressure-treated wood, your equine termite will gnaw it to shreds unless you paint it with some foul-tasting substance.

Wooden fencing wouldn't be a good choice if your horse is a cribber or a wood chewer. A cribber will destroy the top boards; a wood chewer can ingest wood splinters.

▲

Posts should always be outside the fence to prevent the boards from coming loose if your horse leans on the fence.

Electric Fencing

Electric fencing costs less than many other types of fencing. Some horsemen advise that simple hot wire fences not be used to separate a pasture from a road, since horses could run through it if they ever got into a real panic.

An electric fence is also useful if you plan on keeping your horse with cattle — hot wire may be a necessity to keep cattle contained.

There are several types of electrified fences. If the fence is readily visible (marked with a 2- to 3-inch-wide ribbon) and your horse properly introduced to it, she'll most likely respect it. If the fence is not clearly visible, it is unsafe for horses. An obvious disadvantage to electric fencing is the fact that the wires only work when electrified. If a storm knocks your power out, your fence isn't going to be effective or safe.

One special type of electric fencing is called *high-tensile fence,* or New Zealand wire. With traditional electric fencing, the wire will break if the horse gets tangled. With high-tensile wire, the fence will not break. As well, this wire is not safe for horses unless there is a sight rail at the top of the fence to make it visible. High-tensile fencing is not a good choice for small areas where a rolling horse might get a foot caught in it. It should always be electrified when used for horses.

PVC Fencing

A variety of fences now are made from polyvinyl chloride (PVC). This type of fencing requires virtually no maintenance and looks new for years. It also "gives" a little if horses bump into it, which can reduce the risk of injury from fencing. However, it's very expensive.

Wire Fencing

One type of wire fencing used with horses — it can even be seen on large Thoroughbred farms — is a "2 x 4 nonclimb" wire fence. It is used with a board at the top, so horses can see it better and don't lean on it. This can be a safe fence even for excitable horses, but it is expensive.

Woven wire fence, also known as farm fence, is probably the most common fence seen in the eastern half of the United States. This fence can be fine for horses, but the posts need to be secure and there should be a hot wire or a board at the top, to prevent leaning horses from bending the fence down.

Diamond-mesh fence was designed just for horses. It is an excellent, safe fence, but it is very expensive to install.

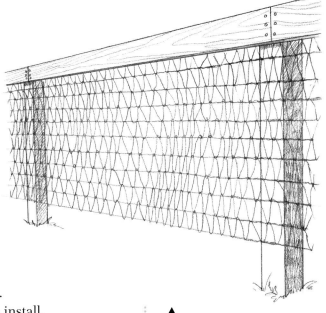

▲
Diamond-mesh fencing is excellent for horses but quite costly.

Steel-Pipe Fencing

A fence made of steel pipe is less costly than a wooden one, especially if used irrigation pipe is available; it should have steel posts. Some maintenance is necessary: It's going to have to be coated periodically with rustproof paint.

Fencing to Avoid

Steer clear of barbed wire. It's very dangerous for horses: If they get caught up in it, they can sustain serious injury.

Even with a well-maintained wooden board fence, a horse may find a way to injure herself. Your job, however, is to build or find a barn with the fence least likely to pose a hazard to your horse.

Feeding

If you're boarding your horse, you will want to find a stable whose manager knows a lot about feeding horses and where the horses are healthy and well fed.

Generally, a good manager will realize that horses should receive some pasture during turnout, plenty of hay, and some grain if they're worked. A good manager also knows that too much grain can make a horse seriously ill. He or she will be a stickler about seeing to it that feed is kept secured so horses can't get into it and eat their fill.

Gates

Gates should be even sturdier than the fence: Horses tend to gather at gates and push, especially around feeding time. Gates should also be easy to operate in all weather. You don't want to be fighting with a gate while you're trying to turn out a rambunctious horse on a muddy day.

A good barn manager knows that a "low-octane" horse, also called an "easy keeper," maintains a good weight with little grain and won't be fed the same way as a "high-octane" horse or "hard keeper." He or she knows, too, that if a horse is receiving less work than usual, her grain should be reduced.

If you locate a terrific barn with an experienced manager, you won't have to worry much about what or how much your horse is being fed. These concerns will be taken care of for you.

If you're planning to feed your horse yourself, though — either at home or at a stable that's not full service — you'll need to learn a lot about feeding a horse in a very short time. (Be sure to read appendix A, Feeding Your Horse.) Feeding a horse inappropriately can have serious consequences. You'll need to know what causes colic and what will cause a horse to develop laminitis or founder, which are serious conditions of the feet that can result from too much rich pasture or grain.

In fact, if you're going solo on feeding your horse, I advise you to surround yourself with experts. Consult with an equine veterinarian, experienced horse owners, and knowledgeable representatives from your local feed store. Feed stores will often send a representative to your home to evaluate your pastures and recommend a complete feeding program to you in writing. This is an invaluable service and should be used, if possible.

Veterinarian and Farrier Care

Enlisting the services of a good veterinarian and farrier is important to the health of your horse. To find the best of these professionals in your area, ask other horse owners. If you ask enough of them, the same names are going to start coming up again and again, and pretty soon you'll have a good idea who provides quality care.

Veterinarian

Good equine veterinarians are worth their weight in gold. If you're keeping your horse at home, make sure your veterinarian and his or her staff are communicative and accessible, since you'll undoubtedly have many questions and concerns when you first take up horsekeeping. You'll also want a veterinarian who can come to your home immediately if you ever have an emergency. A veterinary practice with several doctors on staff might be more accessible than a veterinarian in practice alone, although most veterinarians have someone on call to cover them when they can't be reached.

If you plan on boarding your horse, the veterinarian who services the barn you choose is equally important. Most barns have a "favorite" veterinarian whom they use routinely. If you don't like this person, you should be able to choose a veterinarian with whom you're more comfortable so that you're confident about the care your horse is receiving.

If you're boarding your horse, ask what the barn's policy is on treating sick horses. Some barns won't call a veterinarian until the owner approves the call, which could be detrimental to your horse's health if you're hard to find. The ideal situation is a barn with staff who are able to make good decisions and know when to call the veterinarian.

Know, too, that if your horse has medical insurance, the insurance company usually has to be called anytime a veterinarian sees your horse for anything other than routine care (such as vaccinations). If you don't call, payment might be denied.

Using a different veterinarian, however, may mean you won't be able to cash in on the cost economies often provided when a veterinarian treats an entire stable. Veterinarians charge for a farm call in addition to the cost of whatever special examinations and treatment they provide. If they're coming to see more than one horse, the farm call charge is less.

Some veterinary practices now offer a health plan for horses. A doctor will automatically visit at certain times of year to provide routine health care, such as vaccinations, stool checks, Coggins tests, and, if you like, even worming.

Farrier

A farrier works on horses' feet. Farriers are sometimes called blacksmiths, although some farriers are purists about their title: A blacksmith is anybody who works with iron, but not everyone who works with iron is trained to work on horses' feet. So all farriers are blacksmiths, but not all blacksmiths are farriers.

Whether you're planning on boarding your horse or are going to keep her at home, you'll need the services of a good farrier. If you're on your own and don't know of someone already, ask your veterinarian. He or she will be able to make one or more good recommendations.

If you're boarding your horse, you'll undoubtedly find that the barn has a preferred farrier who's regularly scheduled to come and work on the horses' feet. You need to know who this person is, what the scheduling arrangements are, and how billing is handled. Some barns will require you to be there when your horse is worked on. If your horse won't stand quietly in a cross-tie, a handler may need to be present to hold her and keep her calm. Some barns will handle your horse for you, but may charge you for this service.

If you keep your horse at home, someone must be present when the farrier is there. It isn't safe to leave the farrier alone, because if an accident were to occur, it could be very serious.

If you keep your horse at home, be sure to extend your farrier some "horse" courtesies:

✓ Always make appointments well in advance.

✓ Be on time for any appointment you make. Make sure your horse is in the stable and ready to be shod when the farrier arrives.

✓ For safety's sake, make sure someone in addition to the farrier is always present.

✓ Pay the farrier promptly. Almost all expect payment at the time of service.

When a farrier shoes your horse, he or she cleans and trims the hooves, too, and often can be a good source of information regarding the health of these hooves. He or she can detect thrush and may be able to find an infection. A farrier also routinely examines the old shoes for unusual wear and can often recommend shoeing solutions to some movement problems.

Alternatives to Full Board

Boarding your horse at a barn where the staff worry about everything you don't want to think about is a nice option, but it may be too expensive for you. If so, there are a few other possibilities you might try.

Shared Lease

In a shared lease you lease your horse to another rider or to a stable owner, who may use the horse in lessons. If the arrangement is to split the horse's time 50/50, you'll then pay only half her board. This also means that you get to ride only half as often. With such an arrangement, you need to have schedules worked out well in advance, and it's strongly advisable that you have the terms worked out into a contract (even if you get along fabulously with the person you're leasing your horse to) that should be signed by both parties.

Issues that should be worked out include: who gets to ride on which days; who is responsible for vet bills if the horse gets sick or injures herself; how often the horse is used in lessons, and when.

Co-Op Boarding

A co-op boarding situation is one in which the boarders share the work in order to lower their expenses. This isn't often available to brand-new horse owners, who rarely know enough other owners to form a co-op.

However, if this option arises for you, a co-op can be a fun and less expensive way to board your horse. The co-op makes its own rules. Sometimes one person is assigned to feed all the horses every night for a week, while somebody else handles mornings. Maybe you'll take turns getting the grain or the hay.

Co-ops work well if all the members are willing to put in some hours and stick to the rules. If unreliable people are involved, the whole thing can fall apart quickly and endanger the health of the horses involved.

Self-Service Board

At a self-service facility, you're completely responsible for the care of your horse, including feeding, watering, mucking out stalls, turning her out, blanketing, and anything else she needs. You pay simply to use the facilities.

This option costs far less than other types of boarding arrangements, but it has the same disadvantages as keeping a horse on your own property. You absolutely must be available at least once and probably twice daily to care for your horse. It has the added disadvantage of requiring some driving time, unless you happen to have a neighbor with self-care facilities.

Work for Reduced Board

Sometimes an arrangement can be worked out for boarders to do some work at a stable in exchange for a reduction in board. For example, if you muck your own horse's stall each day and arrive every morning to feed and water her, the stable owner may be able to reduce your monthly board bill.

At other stables, you may be able to reduce your board bill if you work as a stable hand for a certain number of hours a week or on certain days. Before you enter into an agreement such as this, however, be sure you know exactly what the management expects from you and that you're physically capable of performing the work. Also, be sure this type of arrangement will fit your lifestyle; if you're short on time to begin with, adding another commitment may leave you little time to ride.

Planning Ahead

Whether you've decided to keep your horse at home or find a suitable stable, reading this chapter should have made it clear that you'll want to have your horse's accommodations either built (if at home) or carefully selected (if a boarder) well in advance of purchasing her. Don't be tempted, as many first-time horse owners are, to purchase a horse before you've made arrangements for her care!

The time you spend preparing for your new horse is all well spent. If you've done your homework well and made arrangements either at home or at a stable for safe, secure accommodations, you'll be able to fret less and enjoy your horse more. And isn't that what owning a horse is all about?

5

What You Will Need

KEEPING A HORSE REQUIRES EQUIPMENT. Some things you can't do without, and others you can, at least for a while. If you plan to keep your horse at home, you'll need a few more items than if you plan to board him.

There's no doubt about it: Owning a horse is an expensive proposition. Make sure you can afford not just your horse and his upkeep, but also all the gear that goes with him. If you plan and buy carefully, however, you can avoid fretting about the costs and enjoy your new friend!

Tack

Tack is the equipment you'll need to manage your horse on the ground and ride him. You should be able to find everything you need at a local tack shop, or in catalogs that sell horse supplies.

Halter

The halter is a piece of equipment put on the horse's head to enable him to be caught easily, led, or tied. The halter has no bit.

Commercially made halters are usually nylon or leather. If your horse will wear a halter while he's in the stall or out on pasture, it should be a safety or "breakaway" type, which will break if he gets hung up. Nylon won't break, nor may regular halters made of heavy leather.

It's a good idea to own more than one halter. You might want to have one nice new model to put on your horse when you're leading him around, and, if he's turned out with a halter, two breakaways. This way, you'll have a back-up breakaway if one breaks or gets lost or stolen.

Untangling Halters

To the uninitiated, a halter looks like a Chinese puzzle, especially if it's twisted. To help you keep it straight, remember that horse equipment always buckles on the *left* side of the horse. If there's just one buckle, arrange for it to be on the left as you hold the halter. From there, decide where the horse's nose fits. The long pieces of the halter run up the cheeks and over the top of his head, behind the ears.

Halters also have a piece that fastens under the throat. This piece may have a snap that connects to the left cheek piece, or it may be sewn to the left cheek piece. Halters with a snap at the throat are especially easy to slip on and off the horse, as long as the snap is in good condition.

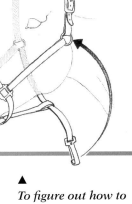

▲
To figure out how to get the halter on, put the buckle on the left; from there, figure out where the horse's nose fits in.

Lead

A lead is a rope, nylon, or leather line with a snap on one end. It will give you control when you lead or handle your horse. Even if you're only going a few feet with him, always lead by using a shank instead of hanging onto his halter. It gives you much better control, is much more pleasant for the horse, and is much safer for you.

Lead lines can be made of many materials, including cotton rope, nylon rope, flat nylon, leather, or combinations of any of these with a length of chain. Leads with chains are not safe for tying horses, and leather leads don't tie well. Leads with chains are useful for controlling a horse that's difficult to lead, however; the chain is run over the nose or under the jaw for extra control. Ask someone knowledgeable to show you how to properly position a chain over or under the nose.

Nylon ropes are very strong and generally tie well. Flat nylon leads, however, can cause rope burns on your hands if your horse jerks suddenly, so opt for the round version.

Always look for a lead with a good stout snap that's easy to operate. If it takes both hands to open the snap, as it does with stout bull snaps, you won't have a free hand to steady your horse as you attach the lead; he could just wander off. The most durable snaps are solid brass, but many useful models are made of lighter metal.

As with halters, it's a good idea to own two leads. Leads get lost, stolen, and broken. You'll want one in reserve so you aren't leadless, because it's an important piece of equipment.

◄
A lead with a chain is useful for controlling a horse while you're walking him, but it should never be used to tie a horse.

◄
Make sure the lead you buy has a snap that can be managed with one hand, such as the one shown here.

Bridle

The bridle enables you to control your horse while you're riding him. Most bridles are meant to be used with a bit; those without bits are generally known as hackamores (see the illustration under Bits).

Bridles are traditionally made of leather, but recently nylon models have become fairly common. They're relatively inexpensive but, as I've said before, nylon won't break. If your horse gets a nylon bridle hung up on something or steps on nylon reins, he could be injured.

Be aware that with many new bridles, the bits aren't included in the price; sometimes the reins aren't, either. Make sure you know what you're getting, especially if you're ordering from a catalog.

Bridle costs range from a few dollars to hundreds for handmade show models. What you'll need to spend largely depends on what you plan to do. For everyday riding, you don't need — or even want — fancy show equipment. Buy sturdy, functional equipment instead that's built to last. And try to avoid cheap leather, which may not hold up. A good-quality used bridle would probably be a better choice than a new one of very cheap leather.

▲

A horse with a typical English bridle (top), and one with a typical Western-style bridle (bottom).

Bits

Many horsemen believe that if a horse requires a severe bit, he isn't trained well. Thus, aim to get your horse to wear a mild bit. If you're true to this goal, you and the horse should be able to advance in skill using just this one, mild bit.

It's true that any bit can be severe in the wrong hands. But it's also true that some bits are inherently milder than others. With the latter type, you'll have a much wide margin for error before you cause your horse discomfort or pain.

Bits have a mouthpiece, either jointed or solid. It may be relatively straight across or mildly curved, or it may have a giant hump in the middle. The gentle arch is called a tongue release. The giant hump is called the port of the bit. The sides of the bit, where it's attached to the rest of the bridle, are called the cheek pieces. If the bit has side pieces that connect to the reins below the mouthpiece, these are called the shanks of the bit.

Bits work on either one or both of two different principles: by pressure on the corners of the horse's mouth, or by putting leverage against the bars (the mandibular, or jaw, bones) of the horse's mouth. Here's some more information on all three types.

Snaffles

Snaffles are usually the mildest of bits. Some people (especially in Western riding circles) believe that a snaffle is any bit jointed in the center. Strictly speaking, however, any bit that works by exerting pressure on the corners of the horse's mouth is a snaffle, whether it's jointed or not.

The thickness of the bit is important. The narrower the bit, the more severe it is. A wire snaffle is an extremely severe bit. A plump, hollow mouth, jointed snaffle is commonly used by English riders. It's comfortable for the horse and, in reasonable use, isn't severe. This bit is hollow to keep its weight down. Another common bit, the rubber snaffle, works well for many horses; just be careful that it's not too fat.

A snaffle that's not jointed but instead gently curved to allow space for the tongue is called a *mullen mouth snaffle*. In a moderately fat form, even in rubber, this is a nice comfortable bit for many horses, although it's considerably harder to find than its jointed cousin. A perfectly straight bar bit is considered quite severe, because it keeps pressure on the tongue.

If you get a Western snaffle (that is, one with shanks), buy one with the shortest possible shank. More length means more leverage, which means the bit is more severe.

Some Western snaffles are jointed in multiple places and move so much that you could find it hard to give your horse consistent signals. I'd stay away from these.

Curbs

Unlike the snaffle, some bits work by putting leverage pressure against the bars of the horse's mouth. Bits with shanks work by leverage pressure. They're used with a strap or a chain that fits under the horse's jaw, and are properly called curb bits.

The word *curb* seems to be shunned by many catalogs that sell bits, however — especially Western bits. Even though many Western bits fall into the category of "curb," they're given different names, such as "performance horse bits."

If you use a curb bit, stay away from the models called "cathedral bits," "headsetters," or "collector bits," which are far too severe, particularly for new horse owners. Bits such as these can be very painful for your horse. A better choice is a curb bit with a low, gentle port and very short shanks. These bits come in a variety of names, depending on the vendor. Sometimes they're called "pleasure curbs." However, if you ride Western but aren't showing your horse in a class that requires a curb bit, I recommend a pleasantly plump English-type snaffle. Your horse will appreciate it.

Full Bridle

In some types of English riding, particularly saddleseat and advanced dressage, you'll see bridles that have two bits: a little snaffle (sometimes called a bridoon) and a curb. This arrangement is properly called a full bridle, and it should only be used by advanced riders with light, skilled hands.

Combination Bits

There's a third, small category of bits: those that can work under either of the above principles. That is, they can work on the corners of the mouth, or they can work by leverage pressure. The English bit called a *Pelham*, used with double reins, is one such bit. When the top rein is engaged, the bit puts pressure on the corners of the mouth; when the bottom rein is used, the bit works more like a curb. The *Kimberwicke* is another bit that can work on either principle.

Selecting a Bit

Select the mildest possible bit that will still allow you to control your horse. Generally, the fatter the bit, the milder it is. If it takes on the dimensions of an overstuffed Polish sausage, however, it may be mild, but it'll also

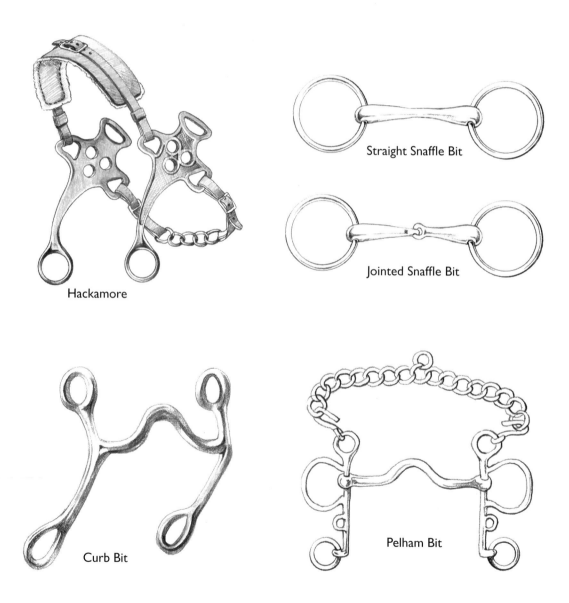

Hackamore

Straight Snaffle Bit

Jointed Snaffle Bit

Curb Bit

Pelham Bit

be uncomfortable for your horse. Conversely, of course, the thinner the bit, the more severe it is. A single-wire snaffle, for instance, is a very harsh bit.

An adult should be able to ride a safe, calm, suitable horse in a fattish snaffle. A child, or someone with a physical disadvantage, might need a little more hardware, perhaps a mild pelham or a very mild curb.

The bit should be wide enough to fit in the horse's mouth without pinching at the corners. For the average horse this will be about 5 inches wide. Very big horses will need more width, and ponies or narrow-muzzled horses, such as some fine Arabs, might need less.

Saddles

Your saddle will probably be your largest expense (other than the horse himself), so put some time and effort into getting the right one. A new, good-quality saddle can be very expensive. But there's a good market for used saddles, and for used children's saddles, which you can use until you're ready to move up and resell. These can be had much more reasonably.

Saddles are personal items. A well-made saddle may fit one rider well and not fit the next rider at all. You need to sit on a lot of them until you find one that fits you. If you're new to horses, experienced tack store personnel can help you learn to feel what's right and what isn't.

But the saddle has to fit your horse, too. If it doesn't, he could develop a sore back and a grouchy temperament. Fitting the saddle to the horse is something far too few people know much about. To learn more about it — and you should — rent a tape from or go to a clinic held by a saddler. The saddlers at clinics would like to sell you one of their saddles, but they're also happy to teach you a great deal in their clinics and tapes even if you don't buy from them initially. They figure if they teach you well, you might be one of their customers in the future.

Fitting a Saddle

Making sure that a saddle fits the horse you use it on is important. The pommel should clear the withers so that the withers don't get pinched and the saddle doesn't interfere with your horse's movement. No part of the saddle should touch the horse's spine directly. In fact, with English saddles, you should be able to see light under the saddle all the way down your horse's spine. Some English saddles are cut back at the pommel to clear the withers.

It's always a good idea to get a saddler or an expert horseman to tell you if a particular saddle fits your horse. A saddle with enough room at the pommel may still pinch at the top of the shoulder blades and cause the horse extreme discomfort. It takes an expert to really show you how to fit a saddle properly.

English Saddles

To the novice, English saddles all look pretty much the same, but this is far from the truth. You can begin to see the differences if you look through any catalog. Some have side flaps that are nearly vertical; others are decidedly sloped. Some have shallow seats, some deep.

What you want is a saddle designed for the kind of riding you'll be doing. An all-purpose saddle is best if you plan on different kinds of riding — perhaps trail riding, some dressage, and even some jumping.

A dressage saddle isn't cut as far forward as the all-purpose is; also, its flaps are longer and its stirrups longer, because your legs are farther back when you ride dressage. A dressage saddle concentrates your weight in the center of the horse's back and is not good for trail riding.

If you're going to focus on jumping you may want a jumping saddle, which is cut farther forward to match the jumping position. But there's a disadvantage to saddles designed exclusively for jumping, especially those called "close-contact" saddles: The seat is so shallow that new riders may have difficulty staying in the middle. A close-contact saddle is really made for experienced show riders. Your saddle should be a help, not a hindrance. You might be better off to select a model with a slightly deeper seat and some support under your knees. Ask your instructor.

Another type of English saddle is the flat saddle, which is used in the show ring for such horses as American Saddle Horses. It's probably not the saddle you'll want for general-purpose riding. It would be a good option if you plan to show in English Pleasure classes on Morgans, Arabs, Saddlebreds, or Walking Horses.

Saddles are traditionally made of leather, although there are synthetics on the market, which are comparatively inexpensive. Many people find

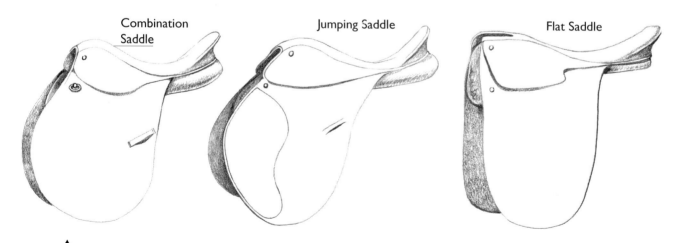

▲
Buy a saddle designed for the type of riding you plan to do. An all-purpose or combination saddle is designed for riders who'll be doing different types of riding. Jumping saddles are designed specifically for the forward-riding position this sport requires. The flat saddle is used on American Saddle Horses and on other breeds in competitions.

these extremely comfortable as well. They haven't been around long enough to rate them thoroughly for durability.

New English saddles are routinely sold "less fittings." This means that you'll have to buy the girth, stirrup leathers, and stirrup irons separately. Get the best-quality fittings you can afford so they won't break while you ride.

If you buy a used saddle, have an expert check to see whether the girth attachment, called the billets, is in good condition. This is crucial: If your billets break, you're going into the dirt. Also have the expert make sure the tree, which is the foundation that the leather of the saddle lies upon, is not cracked, broken, or twisted. A broken tree can hurt your horse, or you.

After you buy a saddle, routinely check the condition of its billets, girth, and leathers. Never skimp on safety items. Don't delay important repairs.

English Saddle Pads

English saddle pads are made to fit particular saddle styles. If you have a forward-seat saddle, for instance, get a pad designed for it. A dressage saddle pad is cut to accommodate the style of a dressage saddle.

Pads may be made of a variety of substances. Synthetic fleece is common. It's also washable and pretty durable, and gives an acceptable amount of protection with a good-fitting saddle. Quilted saddle pads are often seen in the show ring. They don't give as much protection to the horse's back as fleece, and some can be inclined to slide out of position, which you don't want for long-distance riding. Real sheepskin pads are available; these are expensive and hard to clean, but give good protection the horse's back.

There are also specialty pads. Lift-back pads, for instance, raise the back of the saddle a bit to give the rider a better appearance in the show ring, or a slightly better position on some horses. And exotic pads made of new Space Age materials are designed to protect the horse's back, or keep it cool. Specialty pads cost more and it's unlikely you'll need one unless you or your horse have some special problem. If so, your instructor or trainer can recommend a special pad.

Western Saddles

Like English saddles, Western saddles vary widely and are designed for different types of Western riding.

Equitation saddles will cause you to sit in a more upright position than other types. You'll look nice in the show ring, but this saddle will also concentrate your weight onto a pretty small area of the horse's back. For this reason, it's not an ideal general-purpose saddle. The horse may get a sore back if you go on trail rides in one of these.

"Pleasure" or "versatility" saddles might be a better choice for general-purpose riding. Some are designed just for cutting; some have a seat that's longer and flatter to permit you to shift your weight from front to rear. Reining saddles are designed to make it easy to balance. If you don't know

> ### Try It Out
>
> If it's at all possible, test any saddle you're considering on your horse while you ride. This is one of the best ways to ensure the saddle is comfortable for both you and him.

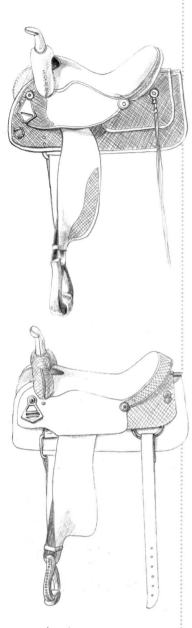

▲
A Western pleasure saddle (top) and a cutting saddle (bottom).

quite what you want to do, these might be a good option. Ask your instructor what types to look at.

Like their English cousins, synthetic Western saddles are available and, in my experience, get good marks for rider comfort as well as low cost. One drawback is that synthetics are scoffed at in the show ring. Again, though, it's a bit too soon to rate them for durability. They come in children's as well as adult sizes.

If you're going to show your Western horse, it would be wise to find out what's currently being seen in the show ring before you invest in a saddle. Sometimes saddles with a lot of silver are in fashion; sometimes they're very much out. You might think you're getting a great deal on a saddle only to find it's so out of style that you feel foolish in the show ring. Style shouldn't count as much as function and fit, but you'll want to find a saddle that offers all three, if possible.

Western saddles come with stirrups, but you may have to buy a cinch separately.

Western Saddle Pads

Western saddle pads include traditional saddle blankets, something that's a cross between a blanket and a pad, show models that look like expensive carpeting, and beautifully handwoven rugs. Show saddle pads can cost hundreds of dollars, and are so exceptionally beautiful your horse will look like a million dollars in one. If you use less expensive, utilitarian pads, you may need more than one. Be careful that any pads or blankets don't slip out of position and that they provide sufficient protection for your horse's back.

Fashions in saddle pads change dramatically from year to year. If you think you're headed for the show ring, such things matter. Scope out the show ring before you buy.

Necessary Tack

Here's a list of essential tack for your horse and its approximate cost. Prices are based on equipment of moderate quality — neither the cheapest nor the most expensive — except where otherwise indicated. Prices are also bound to change. I've listed them here as general guidelines only; consult local tack stores and current catalogs for up-to-date costs.

Regular halter	$20	Bit (jointed snaffle)	$ 20
Breakaway halter (if horse will be turned out with halter on)	$15	Saddle (good-quality used or less expensive new), plus fittings	$600
Lead rope	$ 6	Saddle pad	$ 30
Bridle, including reins	$70	**Total Cost for Initial Tack**	**$761**

Grooming Equipment

You'll need a small assortment of brushes and other grooming tools for your new horse. If you're short on cash, buy just what you need to get the horse groomed routinely, then slowly add to your collection as you're able. Don't forget to let relatives know that extra grooming equipment makes a great birthday or holiday gift!

Grooming your horse is pleasant for both of you. It's also a time to check for skin abrasions and lumps and bumps on legs that may have developed since you last rode. It provides an opportunity to practice ground training your horse to "move over" or "pick up a foot." And it's a time when your horse can get used to the way you talk, the way you move around — and vice versa.

Groom your horse before you ride or work him. This includes picking out his feet. After your ride, wipe him off or brush again as necessary.

Here are the essentials you'll need for grooming and their approximate prices; again, these costs are approximate and likely to increase over time.

Stiff body brush	$ 5
Soft body brush	$ 8
Rubber curry	$ 2
Mane comb (metal is the most durable)	$ 1
Hoof pick	$ 1
Sweat scraper	$ 2
Shedding blade	$ 8
Big sponge (natural sponges rinse out most easily but cost the most; less expensive synthetic sponges are available)	$ 8
Towels (everybody has some old ones that can go to the barn)	$ 0
Scissors*	$12
Total for Grooming Tools	**$47**

Note: Scissors come in handy for cutting bandages as well as for minor trimming jobs.

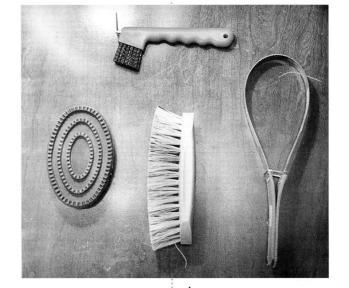

▲
A hoof pick, shedding blade, body brush, and a rubber curry are essentials for grooming (listed clockwise from top).

Clippers

Clippers aren't a must, but they're nice to have if you want to make your horse look especially neat. Clipping may be necessary if you're going to show. If you can't afford to buy clippers, see if you can borrow them as needed; or perhaps you can find a riding friend and split the cost of a pair.

There are clippers for many occasions. When you're shopping, read labels carefully; they'll tell you what the clippers will and won't do. For instance, the smallest and most lightweight are designed just for trimming

▲

Clippers are a great way to neaten up a horse, but they aren't a necessity unless you're going to show.

around the ears or clipping the muzzle. They're fairly inexpensive. They won't hold up to manes or general clipping.

In the mid-price range are clippers that can be used on manes and legs. These are the most practical type for many owners.

At the other end of the scale are heavy-duty clippers you can use to body-clip; if your horse has a heavy coat body-clipping can reduce his cooling-down period after workouts. These clippers can be expensive.

Clippers must be cleaned often, and blades have to be replaced. Various types require special care. For instance, some blades have to be oiled routinely.

Relatively new on the market is a clipper that has a motor separate from its clipper. The hand piece rarely gets hot and it runs smoothly. The blades stay sharp longer because the motor is so powerful. Unfortunately, these clippers cost as much or more than big body clippers.

Grooming Routine

There's no one right way to groom a horse as long as you accomplish your basic goals: to clean his coat of excess dirt, check for any wounds that need treatment, and pick out his feet. Until you develop your own routine, here's a simple one you can follow:

1. Restrain the horse appropriately.
2. Use a rubber curry in gentle, circular motions to loosen dirt, then follow with a medium-stiff brush to whisk the dirt away. Limit use of the curry to above the knees.
3. Use a stiff brush to get dirt off below the knees.
4. Follow using a soft brush to get off fine dust. Use this brush to gently brush larger areas of the face; take care not to poke the eyes! Use your hands to rub off any dirt near the eyes.
5. Use a damp sponge to wipe the corners of the eyes, if necessary, and wipe the nostrils free of excess dirt.
6. Comb (or brush) the mane and tail.
7. Pick out the horse's feet.

You may want to use a body brush on the tail, although grooming experts consider this a sin and use only their fingers on the tail. A metal comb may break hairs in the tail but is usually fine for the mane. A pin brush is also an excellent choice for the tail.

If your horse's coat is caked with mud, use a shedding blade to gently loosen it, then follow the procedure above. Be extra careful with this tool around bony parts.

A horse that's sweaty after a workout on a hot day can be cooled down by rinsing, which you'll want to follow with the sweat scraper to remove excess moisture.

Scissors are handy for trimming the bottom of the tail or behind the fetlock when you don't have clippers or don't want to use them.

Fly-Control Supplies

Protecting your horse from pesky flies and other insects is a must, both when you're riding him and when you're not. The most obvious reason is because insects, especially flies and gnats, can be very bothersome to a horse. They can also spoil a ride, because instead of focusing on instructions from you, the horse will be shaking his head, swishing his tail, and rippling his muscles to keep the flies off. Some insects also transmit diseases, which is just one more reason to protect your horse from them.

The most common method horse owners use to reduce irritation from insects is to spray their animals with an insect repellent daily during warm weather, when the insects abound.

Read labels carefully. Some repellents are ready to use, while others are concentrates and must be mixed with water. You don't want to spray a concentrated solution directly on your horse — you could give him an overdose of insecticide. Concentrates generally are more cost effective, though. Ready-to-use repellents can be purchased by the quart for a moderate price from discount horse catalogs; you may have to buy 3 or 4 quarts to get through one season.

Care must be taken not to get fly spray into your horse's eyes. For the face area, dampen a cloth with some repellent and use the cloth to apply it to the face and ears, or try one of the ready-to-use wipe-on products. (Be aware that some horses develop allergies or reactions to certain fly products; people do, too.) A crocheted ear cover that also has tassels to keep flies off the eyes is inexpensive and nice to use while riding.

Your horse will appreciate a fly mask (fairly inexpensive) while he's in the pasture. If he's seriously bothered by insects despite sprays and even while he's in his stall, you might also want to invest in a scrim sheet, which will help keep flies off him. These sheets are made of mesh so fine that insects can't get through it to bite the horse. They're designed for use at shows or in stalls; most aren't made for turnout. At some very buggy showgrounds, or rest stops on trail rides, fly sheets can be a great blessing.

Blankets

It seems there's a blanket for every purpose and occasion. Whether you need to own any of them depends. If you live in an area that has cold winters, for instance, your horse will grow considerable hair. Some horses are

> ### Medical Supplies
>
> Having some basic medical supplies on hand is a good idea in case your horse sustains a wound or begins to act ill. Here are a few things you should have:
>
> ✓ Antiseptic scrub
>
> ✓ Antiseptic lotion or ointment
>
> ✓ Gauze pads in varying sizes
>
> ✓ Self-adhesive wrap, to hold on gauze pads
>
> ✓ Large animal thermometer
>
> Ask your veterinarian if there are other products you should keep on hand, such as anti-inflammatories or painkillers.

more adept at this than others; ponies are champs at it. If you ride enough to make your horse sweat often in his winter coat and he lives in a stall, not out on pasture, then you probably will need a winter blanket. Lots of winter hair means lots of time carefully cooling him down every time you ride. Blanketing, if you start early enough in the fall, will cause the horse to grow less of a winter coat.

If your horse is stalled, you plan to blanket him, and cooling him off is a problem, you may want to clip all or part of his winter hair. Get somebody to show you how to clip before you try it. But remember: If you cut off the horse's hair and you live in a place with real winter, you *must* blanket him.

Before you sling a blanket up on your horse for the first time, find out how he feels about such things. Some don't care a hoot; some do. Ask his previous owner, if you can; if you can't, ask an experienced horseman to help you try out a blanket initially to see how the horse reacts.

Don't turn your horse outside in a blanket unless it's one designed specifically for turnout. Some blankets are made to be worn only in the stall, and if the horse is turned out in them they can slip, fall around the horse's legs, and panic him.

If you're going to turn your clipped horse outside with a blanket on, you'll need a "turnout rug." These are made for the purpose. They have sturdy leg straps and an outer covering made of canvas or heavy nylon. They can stand up to a rolling horse, to mud, and to rain. But if your horse wears his turnout rug all the time, the leg straps can chafe. In this case you'll want one blanket for inside, another for out.

If you just aren't the type to work your horse hard in the winter very often, or if he lives outside most of the time, let him grow hair. Your horse show friends may snicker at your hairy horse, but the animal will be fine.

Measuring for a Blanket

To figure out what size of blanket your horse wears, measure him from the center of his chest, along the side of his body, straight back to the middle of his tail. This is the same method you'd use to measure a horse for a cooler or sheet.

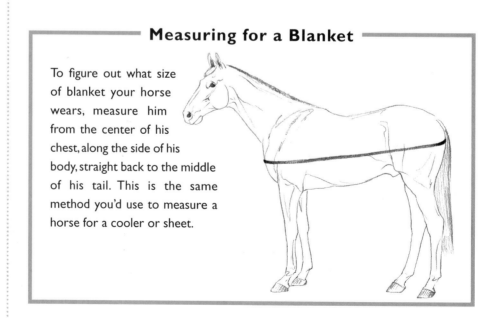

Trim his Billy Goat Gruff beard now and then and brush him, and he'll look bushy but acceptable.

The cost of blankets varies widely. A good-quality blanket, however, should last for many years.

Hoods

In the world of show Quarter Horses, hoods are often used along with blankets. The horses look as if they're forever ready to go jousting. Hoods are thought to cause the hair on the head and neck to stay short and sleek, just as blankets do the hair on the body. Actually, a horse wearing a blanket alone will have neck hair the same length as that of his neighbor wearing a blanket and hood. You just don't need a hood.

Hoods may help keep the mane in place. Still, some horses hate them and will damage their manes as they try to get the hoods off. There are some new devices that a horse can wear to keep his mane in place if you don't want the expense and bother of a hood. They're made of Lycra, come in wild colors, and stay pretty much where they're put.

Sheets and Coolers

Sheets are lightweight blankets, and they're used in stalls to keep horses from getting dirty. Show horses often wear sheets in their stalls in the summer, even between classes, so that they don't get manure stained or covered with bedding. Sheets range from moderately priced to fairly expensive.

Coolers are light blankets that are draped over hot horses as they're walked to cool off. On a hot day, a hot horse will be much better off if you don't cover him with a cooler. Let the air get to him, and hose him down or wipe him off with water. Horses can overheat. On a cold day, however, a hot horse will appreciate a cooler, which can help him lower his body temperature to normal without chilling. Cooler prices depend on their style and material, but are comparable with sheet prices.

An antisweat sheet is made of heavy cotton mesh. The fabric permits the quick drying of moisture on the horse and reduces his cool-off time. The fabric also works a little like a thermal blanket: On a cool day, the antisweat sheet helps hold in heat and, like a cooler, helps prevent chilling. Such sheets are moderately priced.

A cooler helps a horse cool off without chilling after a brisk ride on a winter day.
▼

Bandages

Bandages — the kind used to wrap horses' legs, not the kind used to hold gauze over an injury — and leg wraps, which are like bandages but more substantial, come in endless pretty colors. All the catalogs say they are great for hunt, polo, and race use, so pleasure riders sometimes feel they must need some: Everybody else seems to!

In the beginning, however, bandages probably aren't necessary unless you have a horse with a specific problem. For instance, if your horse grazes one ankle with another foot as he trots or canters, bandages (or boots, discussed below) may be useful. For routine riding on a horse that doesn't hit himself, you don't need them.

Be aware that if put on incorrectly, bandages can cause great harm to your horse and can lead to problems such as a bowed tendon. If you ride through water or heavy dew, bandages can become soaked and fall down, causing a serious tripping hazard to you and your horse. If you plan to ride where this is likely, you'll be better off using boots than bandages.

Sometimes bandages are used in the stall. In some horse realms, notably show hunters and racehorses, this is routine. Bandages protect them from lumps and bumps, and are thought to ease the strain on legs after strenuous workouts. The disadvantage is that some horses come to rely on the bandages for support. Without them, these horses "stock-up," or get fluid in their legs and ankles.

Another disadvantage is that if you bandage every day, small hints of puffiness or heat that might indicate a forthcoming leg problem are masked. The horse may continue in strenuous work when he should be laid off for a few days. By the time a problem surfaces, it's much bigger than it would've been if discovered earlier.

Bandages are useful for shipping; in fact, they should probably be considered a necessity for this purpose. Wrapping the legs protects them in the trailer. Some horsemen prefer bandages, while others like shipping boots.

Wrapping Legs for Trailering

When you're using bandages on your horse's legs for trailering, take care to put them on correctly, because if they slip down they could become entangled in your horse's legs and panic him. So learn how to properly bandage, or ask someone who knows how for help.

If several horses are being shipped in a stock trailer, the danger of one knocking down another's bandages increases; boots, which are less likely to fall down, are a better choice than bandages in this case.

If you do use bandages, they should be applied over leg quilts to provide adequate protection. Be sure to buy bandages with Velcro closures. The other type, bandages with string ties, are slowly disappearing from the market. With string, it's far easier to cause harm to the horse by tying too tight. Furthermore, string tangles and knots and is generally difficult to manage.

A set of four bandages or leg wraps can be purchased from discount horse catalogs fairly inexpensively. Pillow wraps — very thick soft wraps — cost a bit more.

Boots

An alternative to bandages is boots. There are boots for every occasion and they definitely have some advantages. The main one is that they're easier to get on.

Shipping boots offer more protection than bandages. They come in a huge range of shapes and prices, but you can typically obtain a set of four at a moderate price. (Some of the better boots are sold in sets of two, however: Know what you're buying!) The best ones cover not only the lower leg but also the top of the hoof. Most minor trailer injuries are to the area just above the hoof. Some shipping boots have a vinyl outer shell over soft fleece. These work well for most horses, but for those with very fine legs, such as young animals or small Arabs, the vinyl sometimes prevents the boot from fitting well.

Bell boots cover the top of the hoof. They protect the horse from injuries to the coronary band — the area where leg meets hoof — or heels. They're used on horses that step on the heels of their front feet with their hind feet. Bell boots are frequently used by riders who do a great deal of galloping, such as event riders, or those who stop and turn fast, such as contest riders. They're sometimes used when the horse is being shipped. They are almost always used on Standardbred race horses.

Most bell boots are made of something like rubber. They come with many different kinds of closures — including none. These boots pull on, and can be murder until you get the hang of them. Others have Velcro closures, which will fall off in hard going. Those with double Velcro closures will stay on a little better. Still others bell boots have straps and buckles; these get mixed reviews.

Recently some new cushioned bell boots have come on the market. These have an outer covering of brushed nylon. A middle layer is made of the same shock-resistant material used in football helmets; the inner layer is soft and smooth to prevent chafing. The best of these boots are very good because they protect from bruising, but they aren't inexpensive.

There are also boots for every joint and tendon your horse has. Don't buy any of them until you're sure you need them. The most common boot is probably the splint boot, which helps reduce the chance of injury to the splint bone. Splint boots are almost always used by contest riders, and on horses that put a great deal of strain on their legs running and turning. Some people even turn out bouncy horses in splint boots just to prevent accidents. High-tech, multilayered, cushioned, shock-resistant splint boots, or well-made leather ones, are the best, but of course they're the most expensive, too.

Galloping boots give more protection to the tendon at the back of the front leg than do splint boots. High-tech, layered boots are excellent but can get heavy when wet. Good leather galloping boots, or some of the best plastic ones, are other fine choices if these are really necessary.

There are also boots for hocks, knees, and ankles. For light riding you probably won't need any of these.

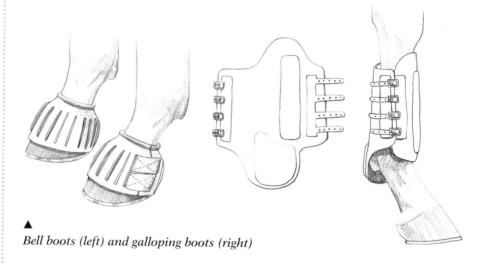

▲
Bell boots (left) and galloping boots (right)

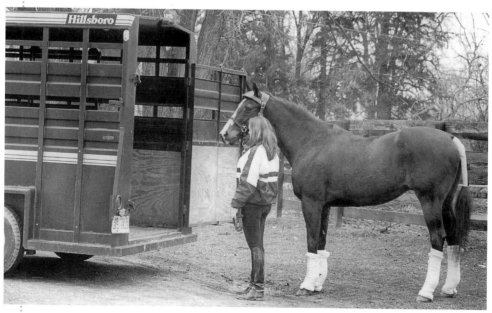

▶
This horse is well protected for trailering.

Longeing Equipment

You may want a longe line. Longeing is a good way to provide exercise for your horse when you can't ride (assuming he knows how to behave on a longe line). If he's been confined to his stall for some reason, for example, longeing is one way to help him expend pent-up energy so he doesn't overdo things and hurt himself when he's finally turned out. Likewise, if he hasn't been ridden for a while and you're concerned that he might be frisky under saddle, longeing before riding will help quiet him down.

Longeing lines generally are 25 or 30 feet long; they're made of nylon or cotton, and are fairly inexpensive. Watch out for flat, thin, nylon longe lines: If your horse pulls, you could get serious rope burn. The lines with a swivel snap at the horse's end are probably the best.

Truck

If you plan to pull a horse trailer, you must have at least a ½-ton truck. Lightweight trucks just aren't made for pulling a trailer. It's extremely dangerous to try it.

Make sure you get a truck with a "towing package," which means it has an oversize cooling system, heavy suspension, and transmission cooler. You'll be sorry one day if you don't.

You'll have to price trucks (and trailers, below) yourself!

Trailer

Horse trailers can be made in a variety of configurations and out of a variety of materials. The standard is probably the steel side-by-side, two-horse trailer. The bad news is that steel rusts if kept outside.

If you're looking at a used trailer, make certain that somebody who knows what to look for climbs under the thing and checks for signs of rust. A cheap used trailer is probably cheap for a reason, such as that it's unsafe. Make sure you don't buy an unsafe trailer.

Also, if you buy a used trailer, *check the floor*. If a pocketknife can easily stick more than ¼ inch into a wooden floor, you need a new floor. Don't take any chances here. Repeat this test on your own trailer at least once a year. Replace the floor immediately if it fails the pocketknife test.

Aluminum Trailers

Although you'll hear endless discussion about this issue, I believe the safest aluminum trailers have a steel frame and aluminum skin. Aluminum frames are lighter, but less durable. Aluminum trailers have very long lives, and of course they don't rust. The bad thing about aluminum is that it's very difficult to weld, and the welds sometimes crack. If a crack occurs somewhere you can't see it, you could have a disaster. This is a bigger problem in very long trailers than in smaller ones, but keep it in mind in any case. If you're looking at an aluminum trailer, new or used, crawl under it to examine every inch, or have somebody else do so. You need to repeat this from time to time after you buy the trailer, too. Cracks in welds are your enemy.

Two-Horse Trailers

Any two-horse trailer you buy should have two axles, and brakes on both axles. It should also be big enough to accommodate your horse without stuffing him inside. He shouldn't be forced to lower his head, or have his rump mashed into the door. And look for signs of rust or, worse, corrosion that has been painted over so you won't notice it.

Trailer Hitch and Sway Bars

If you have a bumper-pull trailer, get top-quality hitch and sway bars. These will add to your cost, but it isn't safe to pull without them. If you know anyone who pulls an Airstream travel trailer, he or she is likely an excellent source of information on hitches and sway control, and where in your area to buy them and have them installed.

▲

It takes skill to haul a horse around in a trailer, so get someone experienced to give you several lessons without a horse aboard, and practice, practice practice! Practice on all types of terrain — not just roads, but also muddy fields like those you might encounter going to horse shows. Braking and backing up should be second nature to you before you actually haul a horse.

Trailer Tires

Tires should be in top condition. Most horse trailer tires are more likely to die of dry rot than to fall apart from overuse: Check them often for signs of rot. This means looking at the sidewalls, not just the tread.

Also, make sure that the tires on any trailer are compatible with the tires on your pulling vehicle. You don't want radials on one and nonradials on the other.

Insurance

You'll need liability insurance. This will cover you should your horse do something rude — such as bite somebody, step on them, or kick them — or if he gets out and damages someone else's property. Ask your insurance agent about what kind of policy you should have to cover these kinds of risks.

Mortality insurance on your horse, which pays you if he drops dead, can be expensive (depending on your perspective), and may come with strings attached. For example, rarely does a horse just drop dead; it's much more common for him to become ill, worsen, and finally have to be euthanized. Your insurance may force you to take your horse to surgery, or prevent you from doing so, depending on the situation. You can't just put the horse down; you must talk to your insurance company first. Be aware that a few less reputable agents are out there, and can be hard to find when you need them most. Still, most companies are reasonable, and customers are glad to have a policy with them when problems arise.

Medical insurance for horses, just as for people, comes with a deductible that you pay before the insurer starts picking up the bills. Then there's a limit on the total amount the insurer will pay. Do be aware of exclusions that come with medical policies. These vary among companies, but a common one is for colic surgery. If your horse survives colic surgery, you may not be able to insure him in the future for this particular problem. For other medical conditions the insurer may pay initially, but exclude that illness during the next policy period until the horse has been free of the condition for a certain period of time, such as six months.

Another kind of insurance is for "loss of use." In theory, this insurance will pay you if your horse is no longer able to be used for the purpose for which he was intended. But you should know that when the company pays you, it takes the horse. Can you deal with this emotionally? This insurance is incredibly expensive, as well. It's most often used for very valuable breeding or show stock.

Be sure you know what you're getting when you buy any type of insurance, and be sure to investigate the company as well as the type of coverage.

Supplies for Horses on Your Property

If you won't be boarding your horse and plan to keep him at home on your own property, here are some additional items you'll need. Remember that bedding, hay, and grain will be ongoing expenses. If you don't have a truck and the strength to pick up and haul supplies yourself, you might also have to pay for delivery of bedding, hay, and grain.

The cost of many of these items will vary depending on where you live and current going prices. Ask other horse owners for current costs:

- ✓ Bedding
- ✓ Hay
- ✓ Grain
- ✓ Water tanks for outside
- ✓ Buckets and feed tubs for inside
- ✓ Pitchfork
- ✓ Rake

You'll also need a wheelbarrow and hose, but if you have the kind of property on which a horse can live, you probably already have these on hand anyway.

6

Safety Around Horses

WHEN YOU OWN A HORSE, you need to learn to see situations that may get you or her into trouble before they occur. Practice looking for potential hazards. It's like the "What's Wrong with This Picture" game you played as a child: If you get good at it and learn to anticipate trouble, chances are you'll never get hurt. A little foresight can help ensure that the time you spend with your horse is happy for both of you.

There's no way I can list all the situations that might come up and tell you what to do about each, but there are some categories of situations that cause problems so often that they need to be mentioned to new horsemen.

Sacred Safety Rules

There are two unbreakable rules you need to remember when you're dealing with horses. Everybody is aware of these concepts on some level, but surprisingly few people regard them as absolute laws that must never ever be broken, no matter what. These sacred laws are best presented by the great horseman John Lyons — a man who has started several thousand horses under saddle and has been smart enough to learn from all of them. If someone as experienced and careful as John Lyons regards these rules as unbreakable, you should, too.

1. *Never* put yourself in a situation where you could be hurt. Nothing is worth your injury.
2. *Never* put yourself in a situation where your horse could be hurt.

As obvious as these rules are, they're easy to forget in times of stress, and those are the times you most need to remember them. Put these rules in your long-term memory and think about them whenever you work with horses.

Be especially conscious of these rules anytime you're about to try something new, whether it be a ground chore such as clipping a horse for the first time or an under-saddle technique in a class with an instructor. Always ask yourself if you could get hurt if you proceed, or if your horse could. If you come up with the wrong answer, don't do it.

Safe Ground Practices

If your experience around horses has primarily been with gentle, well-trained animals it's easy to take their good ground manners for granted and let yourself get lazy about handling horses correctly and safely. Remember, though, that even the best-mannered horses are still horses, and you can get hurt by accident if you aren't paying attention. In addition, you may one day meet an uneducated horse that doesn't know the ground rules. If you always pay attention to the fundamentals of safety, no matter how quiet a horse seems, you'll have far fewer chances for accidents.

Horses don't like surprises. A surprised horse can go off like a bomb and stomp on everybody nearby. Thus, try not to make sudden movements or loud noises around horses. You don't have to creep around in silence; just don't make big unexpected gestures or noises around the animals.

Don't expect your horse to think like you do: For example, don't tie balloons to her tail as a birthday surprise. (This has been done, believe it or not, and unsuccessfully.) Balloons can spook even a usually docile horse, even if they aren't tied to her tail.

Think about what you're going to do in advance so that you can plan ways not to surprise your horse. She'll appreciate it, and this will make your life safer and easier.

Approaching Horses

Always talk to a horse to let her know you're coming, especially if she's facing the other way. Don't just slap her on the rump to announce your presence; use gentle conversation.

Try to approach a horse from the side, toward her shoulder, where she can easily see you. Don't approach from directly in back or in front, where her line of vision isn't as good.

Stall Safety

A horse should be facing you before you enter the stall. Don't go into the stall if her hind end is toward you. A well-behaved horse will turn toward you when you approach and speak to her, although any horse can have a bad day and show you her hind end from time to time. If, however, you need to get a horse you don't know well out of the stall, or a usually well-behaved horse is looking uncharacteristically grumpy and facing away from you, get someone with more experience to help.

When you're leading a horse into a stall, step ahead of her (you both can't fit through the doorway), then turn circle and turn her completely around to face the stall door before you remove her rope and halter. If you try to let her go through first you could get pulled right into the doorjamb, or she may decide she doesn't want to go in and back out into you.

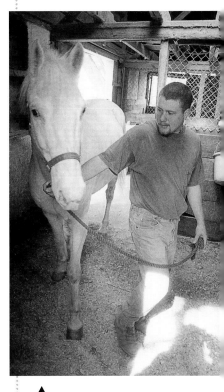

▲
When you're leading a horse into a stall, step ahead of her, then turn circle and turn her completely around to face the stall door before you remove her rope and halter.

Hay Nets

Take care to tie hay nets high enough that your horse can't get a leg through one if she happens to paw. As a horse removes hay from the net, it will sink lower; take this into account when you tie up a full net.

As an alternative, use a hay bag, which has only one opening that the horse can pull the hay through. These bags may be safer than nets and, with most horses, waste less hay.

Avoid the Rear

It really is a good idea never to walk behind a horse, especially one you don't know. Allow about 12 feet of clearance. Even if you're working on the hind end of a well-behaved horse that you know doesn't kick, don't stand directly behind her. If you're grooming the tail, for example, stand to the side of the horse, but stay close to her. This way, if something frightens her and she kicks out, the impact won't be as great as it would be if you were standing 2 feet away.

It's an equally good idea to avoid standing directly in front of a horse. If you're just talking to her, or brushing her face, stand slightly to the side, where she can more easily see you.

Extra Safety Tips for Grooming

If you're grooming a horse that's tied or in cross-ties, never put your arms over the rope or ropes restraining her. If she jerks up, you could be injured.

Always be conscious of the horse's behavior and reactions while you're grooming. Watch for laid-back ears or other signs that she's irritated by something; figure out what's wrong and try to correct the problem, or get help.

Tying

Tying has probably resulted in more harm to horses and people than any other single activity. Before you tie a horse, ask if she's "broke to tie." This expression means that a horse is well trained to tie and will stand patiently and quietly when tied. Horses don't come into the world used to being tied; it takes a great deal of careful and patient training.

If the horse isn't broke to tie, don't try to teach her yourself. Enlist someone with experience who is as determined as you are not to get the horse hurt.

If she is broke to tie and you're going to tie her, make sure that your footing isn't slick and that the immediate environment is free from hazards. If a tied horse backs into a pitchfork propped behind her, for example, she could panic and a disaster could result. Move things at least twice as far away from the horse as seems necessary. It's simply amazing how far a horse can wiggle around and get into things you thought were out of the way.

It's also a good idea to make sure you have an easy escape route anytime you're working with a tied horse; even a well-behaved horse can shy.

A horse that's tied should have on a halter with a round nylon rope attached, never her bridle and reins. Ignore what you've seen in cowboy movies: When a horse is tied by her reins, it's almost inevitable that she will pull on her mouth and panic. You'll wind up with either broken reins or a horse with a broken jaw. In either case, the horse will be harder to tie next time.

Use the nylon rope to make a quick-release knot: a knot that you can untie by giving it one quick tug if the horse gets into trouble. Don't use a rope that's got a chain on the end, because the horse could hurt herself, and don't tie a horse with a fat round cotton rope, which won't always easily release from a quick-release knot.

The rope should be relatively short — about the level of the withers or a little above — and the horse should have just enough freedom to move her head and neck around comfortably. The rope shouldn't be so slack that

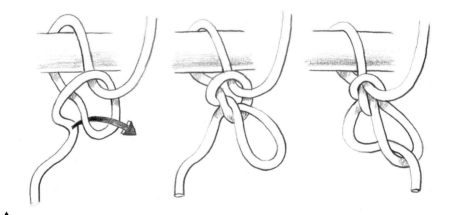

▲

Always use a quick-release knot when you tie a horse.

she can get a leg over it, or twist around and get it hung up around her neck. Don't plan to tie the horse so she can graze while tied; it doesn't work. Sooner or later, she'll get a leg over the rope and break the rope or panic.

Use a really secure object to tie the horse. Corner posts sunk 4 feet into solid ground usually are okay as long as there's no way your horse can paw and get hung up in a connecting or nearby fence.

Tie the horse so her head is at a comfortable, normal height. If you tie her head so low that she can't lift it when she wants, she'll panic. Keep tied horses safely spaced apart to avoid any scuffles. Keep a watchful eye, as well: It's wise never to leave a tied horse unattended.

Places that pose safety hazards to your horse and that are unsuitable for tying include metal fence posts or light wooden posts, which she can easily pull out of the ground, or any post attached to barbed wire, which can seriously injure her. Don't tie a horse to anything like a cinder block; she could pull it along and bang herself in the legs. If you're tying a horse to a horse trailer, take special care about where you tie her. License plates on horse trailers have sliced more than a few legs when tied horses began to paw. Know, too, that a horse can pull a horse trailer that isn't attached to a truck, which can cause a real panic. Don't ever tie to one!

Cross-Tying

As with tying to a post, horses must also be trained to stand in cross-ties. Cross-ties are more dangerous than single ties because in cross-ties both sides of the horse's head are secured, which may double the likelihood that the horse will panic. Ideally, you'll be buying a horse that's well behaved and already accustomed to tying or cross-ties.

If you have to accustom your horse to cross-ties, however, start teaching her in a place where nothing can come up behind her and frighten her. You could use her stall if you can position yourself in such a way that you can readily get out if she gives you trouble.

Secure one side of the halter to a cross-tie, and hold a lead shank in your hand on the other side. Then go on with some easy activity, such as grooming. When the horse is comfortable with one cross-tie and you holding the shank, you can go on to tie the second side to a cross-tie when you groom. This could take one session or several weeks, depending on your horse. Let her tell you when she's relaxed enough for the next step. Don't leave her tied there to see how it works out. Be ready to free her if she has a panic attack, but don't get yourself hurt.

Make sure you find out if your horse has been "broke to tie" before you tie her.

Horse-Tying Safety

Make certain when you do tie a horse that:

✓ The horse is broke to tie.

✓ The rope is secured only to a very safe, solid object.

✓ No hazardous objects are nearby.

✓ The horse will be tied at about the level of her withers.

✓ The rope is short enough that the horse can't get a leg over it, but not so short that she can't move at all.

✓ The rope is secured with a quick-release knot.

✓ The rope is made of something that will untie easily if the horse really yanks on the knot, such as nylon.

✓ There's nothing around for the horse to bump into or paw.

✓ There are no other horses close enough to get into kicking wars.

Always avoid cross-tying a horse in a place where something could scare her from behind. This is how accidents happen with cross-ties: A dog, cat, or child scoots through the barn coming up behind the horse. The horse tries to get out of the way, finds that both sides of her head are secured, and panics. The usual response is for her to go straight up. It's thus a good idea to have a wall behind a horse in cross-ties: Nothing can come up from behind and scare her, and she'll be discouraged from sitting back.

If you use cross-ties, always have quick-release snaps, which you can readily release if the horse does panic and rear or sit back. These snaps can prevent your horse from serious injury to her neck if she rears and falls backward.

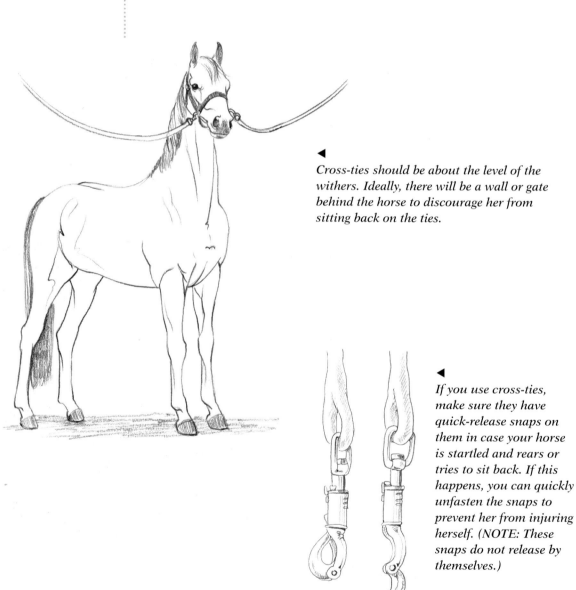

◄

Cross-ties should be about the level of the withers. Ideally, there will be a wall or gate behind the horse to discourage her from sitting back on the ties.

◄

If you use cross-ties, make sure they have quick-release snaps on them in case your horse is startled and rears or tries to sit back. If this happens, you can quickly unfasten the snaps to prevent her from injuring herself. (NOTE: These snaps do not release by themselves.)

Tying in a Trailer

A horse in a trailer must have her rump secured by a butt bar before she is tied. Otherwise she could step back, get her back feet on the ramp or ground, find that her head is tied, and panic. She could seriously injure herself and, at the very least, will be harder to load next time. Use this method for tying your horse in a trailer:

1. Load the horse.

2. Have someone stand at her head. (Only the best-broke horse on earth can be allowed to stand alone.)

3. Secure the butt chain or butt bar.

4. Close the ramp or rear door.

5. Tie the horse's head so that she can move her head and neck, without feeling overly restrained, but also can't get into trouble. Always tie with a quick-release knot, or use a trailer tie with a quick-release in good working condition. *If the horse is not broke to tie, do not tie her in the trailer.*

When you unload your horse, make sure her head is untied before you release the butt bar. When a trailer door opens, nearly every horse in the world will presume it's time to get out. If she's tied, your horse will start to leave, find her head tied, give a good yank, panic, and you'll have a disaster.

Leading

It's tempting to grab a horse by the halter and lead her around instead of taking the time to go get a lead rope, especially if you don't have far to take her, but horses don't like to feel something pulling on their heads. It makes them uncomfortable and, understandably, some horses may yank their heads up in protest. You could easily be injured if the horse pulls, and likewise, the horse could easily escape.

Avoid this by using a lead rope on your horse every time you lead. Make sure children use one, too. You'll save fingers, elbows, and shoulders from potential injury if the horse pulls, and life will be much more pleasant for her, too.

Most horses are perfectly happy to come right along with you if you use a lead; they resist less than if you just grab the halter with your hand. Also, if your horse becomes frightened for any reason while you're leading her, the lead rope gives you a much better chance to regain control than your hand alone does.

▲
When you lead a horse, you should position yourself just in front of the shoulder.

Summing Up
Safe Leading

Follow these procedures when leading:

✓ Always use a lead rope attached to a halter to lead a horse.

✓ Always lead from the shoulder.

✓ Hold the rope several inches under the horse's chin.

✓ Don't wrap the rope around your hands or arms.

✓ Position yourself toward the front of the horse's shoulder.

Most horses are used to being led from the left. Thus as you're leading your horse, you should walk at the front of her left shoulder, whether you're using a lead rope or have her by the reins. She shouldn't get behind you or too far in front. Hold the rope or reins several inches under her chin. Never let a rope get wrapped around your hand, arm, or any other part of your body. If the horse tends to crowd you as you walk, push her away with your right elbow.

Holding a Horse for Someone Else

Holding a horse is one of those jobs that looks like the easiest thing in the world. If you don't pay attention every moment, though, things can go to pieces in a flash.

If you're holding a horse for someone like the farrier or veterinarian, always stand on the same side of the horse as this person. This is especially true if the other person is working on the hind end. If you have to make a correction and tug on your horse's lead shank, you'll be pulling her head toward you, and her hind end will swing the other way — not into the person working on her.

Always pay strict attention to what's going on when you hold a horse for someone. Keep your eyes on the horse, not on the farrier or veterinarian, no matter what he or she is doing! The quietest horses can have bad moments when a cat jumps out of the rafters or a door slams, and they can hurt anybody who isn't paying attention. Never take this job for granted.

Turning Out

Make sure your horse is well behaved and doesn't try to take off as she nears the gate when you go to turn her out to pasture. If she's not well trained in this regard, enlist a knowledgeable person to help retrain her for turnout. Be consistent, and never let your horse loose until she behaves.

Safe Treat Tips

Don't carry treats, grain, or hay into a pasture that holds more than one horse. You could find yourself in the middle of a scuffle. Give your horse her treat before you get there (or after you get her out).

When feeding your horse a treat such as a carrot or piece of apple, be sure to hold your hand completely flat so she doesn't accidentally nip a finger or two. Some lesson barns won't even let their horses be fed by hand; they require treats to be served in a bucket.

Give small treats. Break up large pieces of carrot, and cut small apples in half and large apples into quarters before serving; otherwise, they could lodge in your horse's throat.

Assuming your horse is well behaved, walk her through the gate, shut the gate behind you but don't lock it, then turn her to face you before releasing her. You want to reinforce the good habit of having her wait to be released before she trots off to enjoy turnout. *Watch your horse every second!* Move away from her as soon as she's set free. A happy horse might literally kick up her heels.

If you're turning a horse out into a pasture where other horses are congregating near the gate, carry a whip (if it won't bother your horse) to wave the other horses off while you turn out your horse. Or enlist the help of someone else to shoo away other horses so you can turn yours out.

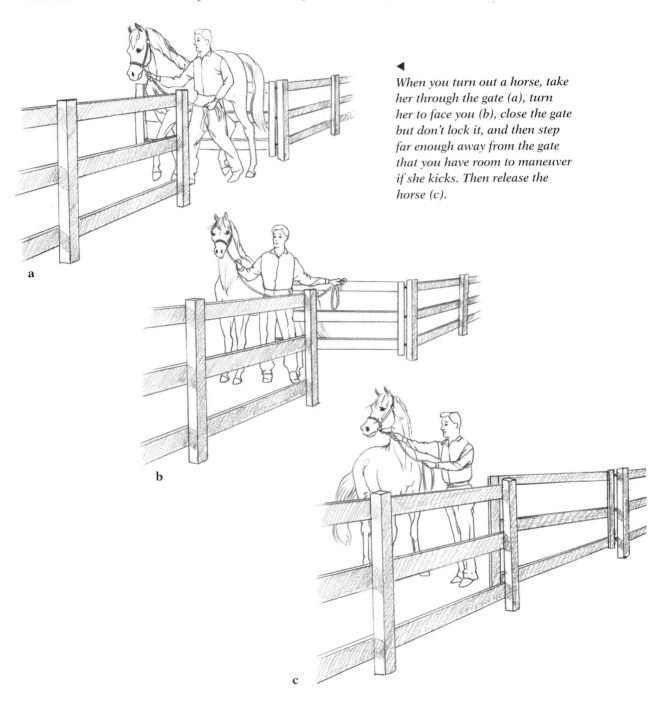

◄

When you turn out a horse, take her through the gate (a), turn her to face you (b), close the gate but don't lock it, and then step far enough away from the gate that you have room to maneuver if she kicks. Then release the horse (c).

a

b

c

Safe Riding

You're in charge of the basics of your own safety when you're riding. There's always some inherent danger when you ride horses; for some people this is part of the fun. But you can minimize unnecessary danger by making sure you're well equipped with a helmet and other safe riding equipment.

Check Your Tack

Before you climb on a horse, check the saddle and bridle for dangerous cracks in the leather, ripped or missing stitching, loose or broken buckles, unsafe stirrup leathers, and things that aren't put together correctly. It doesn't have to take you all day to give your equipment the once-over. Still, a quick check is important: In some less elegant riding moments, all that may be keeping you from a trip into the dirt is your saddle and bridle. It makes sense to be sure they aren't about to fall apart right when you need them.

Do this routinely so it becomes a habit. It's too easy to get into the habit of *not* checking tack routinely.

Safe Riding Attire

Beginning riders and pleasure riders don't need much in the way of special riding clothes, but two musts are a helmet and sturdy shoes.

Helmet

Since we're only issued one head per lifetime, it makes sense to use it well and wisely. For riders, that means wearing a helmet every time you're on a horse, whether you're riding for a minute or an hour. Your life really could depend on wearing a safe helmet. This should not be something you even question: Always wear a helmet.

If you're not used to wearing a helmet, it will feel odd the first couple of times you put one on. But you'll soon get so used to it that you'll feel exposed without one. Remember, serious head injuries are often cumulative; a few unprotected bumps can add up to a very serious lifelong problem.

Not all helmets sold in tack stores today are adequate to protect your head while riding. Be sure to buy one that is ASTM/SEI approved. This means the helmet has met certain safety standards.

If a helmet fits well, it should be comfortable but sit securely on your head. It shouldn't become displaced if you shake your head forward and backward or from side to side.

Shoes

A good general rule is that you should wear sturdy shoes or boots when you work around horses. Don't wear sandals, for obvious reasons.

▲
This rider is dressed safely, with protective helmet and sturdy riding boots.

Nowadays, many people wear sneakers around the barn. This isn't preferred foot gear, although it's so common that riding sneakers are sold for the purpose. Sooner or later, however, sneaker-clad people will be stepped on and regret their choice.

In the opposite camp are some people so determined to protect their toes that they wear steel-toed shoes. These can be a hazard in themselves: If a horse tromps hard on the steel toe, the steel will bend, which could cut or even sever your toe.

Opt for sturdy shoes or boots with a heel to keep your foot from going through the stirrup. Avoid footwear with material on the sole that might keep your foot from coming out of the stirrup easily if you fall off.

Check Your Girth

No matter who saddled a horse for you, always check the girth just before you get on. Many horses inhale air when the girth is put on; when they relax, the girth goes loose.

After you ride for 5 or 10 minutes, check the girth again. Check it one more time after you've been riding for a while, especially if your horse has sweated up. Remember, you're in charge of your own life and safety. Always check the girth.

Riding Wise

It's always best to ride with others so that if one person has a problem, the others can go for help. If you do ride alone at least file a "flight plan," so someone knows which way you went and when you should be back. Here are other important tips to keep you and your horse safe:

✓ Watch the footing! Don't ride if it's icy or muddy; this can lead to slips and injuries.

✓ Check out unknown terrain. For example, before you take your horse across a field that you aren't certain is safe, slowly walk her across a chosen path, watching carefully to make sure there are no groundhog holes she could step in, there's no barbed wire on the ground, and there are no other places she could injure herself. It's especially important to check out the terrain before trotting, cantering, or galloping across a field.

✓ Only cross water where other riders have safely done so before. These are likely to be small-creek crossings along the trails you use. Don't try to cross at new places unless you're certain it's shallow and safe. Also, if your horse refuses to cross, don't push her. For an inexperienced rider this could be a dangerous situation.

✓ If you have to ride on a road or across driveways, go at a slow walk. Pavement can be slippery!

Walk Toward Home

Although it seems pretty obvious, there are always newcomers who don't know the rule: Don't trot, canter, or gallop toward the barn. A lot of horses will become uncontrollable in their efforts to race back to the barn, and perhaps scrape you off on the barn door. Never take this chance; don't let your horse get in the habit of hurrying toward home.

Jewelry and Hair

Hoop earrings can snag easily on just about anything, including a leafy twig or your shirt if you rub your face on your shoulder. If your horse rubs against you, her bridle or mane may also catch in your earrings.

It's wise to wear no earrings at all or, if you must, small posts that lay flat on your ear when you're around horses. In fact, this is a rule in the hunt field and among show hunters. Rings also snag easily; leave them at home when you ride, too.

If you have long hair, it can blow in your face at the wrong time and you can miss seeing something important. Tie your hair back, or braid it.

7

Horse Health

IT'S BEYOND THE SCOPE OF THIS BOOK to tell you all the medical problems that might come up during horse ownership. Still, I have listed some of the most common ones below. It's important that you know something about problems that require a call to the veterinarian. A little knowledge of what's not normal could save your horse's life.

Bowed Tendon

This is a serious injury to one or more of the major tendons that run down the back of the horse's lower leg. A true bow involves damage to the fibers of the tendon itself. When a horse bows a tendon, he has torn or harmed his superficial flexor tendon, deep flexor tendon, or both. The initial injury is very painful. The horse will often refuse to bear any weight on the injured leg. There will be heat and swelling along his tendon.

Bowed tendons usually affect one of the front legs and are more likely to occur in horses used for strenuous and fast sports such as racing, barrel racing, and jumping. It's unlikely that a horse will bow a tendon during pleasure or trail riding, but any horse can bow a tendon horsing around in the field.

If your horse goes lame and this type of injury is a possibility, call a veterinarian promptly. If your horse goes lame while you're riding and you suspect he might have bowed a tendon, get off immediately, lead him slowly to the nearest place he can get on a trailer, haul him home, and call the veterinarian. Don't make him walk any farther than absolutely necessary.

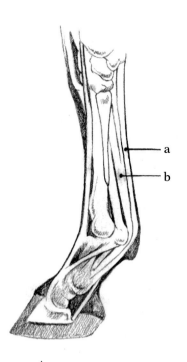

▲

A bowed tendon is an injury to one or more of the major tendons that run down the back of the horse's lower leg: the superficial flexor tendon (a) and the deep flexor tendon (b). Usually, the front legs are affected.

The best thing you can do for your horse until the veterinarian arrives is hose his leg with cold water for a half hour or more. Don't exercise him, put heat of any kind on the area, or put anything on his leg that is supposed to "tighten tendons" or reduce swelling. These products are not for use on a new injury.

A bowed tendon often requires the horse to be rested for six months to a year. Even then, some horses will never be able to return to anything but the very mildest exercise, unless they have surgery. The best surgery for bowed tendons is pretty new, so not all veterinarians are equally skilled at it. The severity of the injury and the time between the injury and the surgery are important factors in determining how well, or if, your horse will recover.

After a horse with a bowed tendon has been rested, his leg will often look substantially thicker than a normal leg. As you look at the leg from the side, the tendon will often have a dished or bowed appearance.

Bandage Bow

Another type of bow is called a bandage bow, or cording bow. In this case, something has been tight enough around the leg to cause injury to the tendon. For instance, if leg bandages are put on too tight or held on with strings that are too tight, it's possible to cause a bandage bow. The prognosis needn't be too bad if a bandage bow is discovered fairly soon after it happens, the leg is hosed, and the horse rested for a period of time determined by the veterinarian.

Most of the time, the bandage wasn't on so tightly that it permanently injured a great deal of the tendon. Still, it's better to prevent bandage bows in the first place: Learn how to bandage your horse correctly.

Choke

Choke means food is blocking the horse's esophagus. Signs of choke include an extended head and neck; sometimes, bits of food may come out the horse's nose. The horse also may slobber excessively.

Some horses with choke will clear the blockage themselves, but if you suspect your horse has this problem, call the veterinarian immediately. Don't try to squirt anything into the horse's mouth; it could go to his lungs, because he won't be able to swallow.

Colic

Colic is an unspecific word that means the horse hurts somewhere in his digestive tract. It's roughly equivalent to the term *stomachache* in people. Like stomachaches, which can be due to anything from a little indigestion

When to Call the Veterinarian

If your horse is lame or sustains a serious wound, it's pretty obvious you need to call the veterinarian. But with other potentially serious conditions, the symptoms may be more subtle. Some indicators that your horse is ill and requires the attention of a veterinarian follow. If you aren't sure, call your veterinarian, report the signs, and ask for advice.

✓ Loss of appetite (refusal to eat grain, hay, or treats)

✓ Depression (hangs head, acts lethargic)

✓ Excessive shivering or inappropriate sweating

✓ Lying down for more than short periods of time

✓ Rolling in distress

✓ Tossing head toward flank

✓ Elevated temperature (normal is 101°F)

✓ Odd standing position

✓ Coughing

✓ Discharge from eyes or nose

✓ Straining while urinating

✓ Diarrhea or change in appearance of stool

✓ Failure to pass stool

to something far more serious, the cause of colic in a horse can range from minor gas to a life-threatening intestinal impaction.

Unfortunately, the signs of discomfort don't always indicate the gravity of the underlying problem. In other words, a horse with signs of colic may not seem to be in great distress, but he can still have a serious problem. Colic also happens to be a leading cause of death in horses, so be well informed about the signs of colic and how to proceed.

Signs of Colic

Some colicky horses will lie down quietly and look vaguely depressed. If you notice your horse lying down at a time of day he's usually up on his feet, make him get up. If he goes back down right away, call the veterinarian.

Some colicky horses will look at their sides, bite at their sides, or kick at their bellies. If you see this going on for 15 or 20 minutes, call the veterinarian. Do the same if a horse looks sweaty and distressed when it isn't hot and he shouldn't be sweating; these, too, could well be signs of colic.

Some colicky horses will roll repeatedly. It shouldn't take long for you to notice the difference between a horse that feels good taking a roll in the dirt because his back itches and one that's rolling because he's in discomfort. Some horses in pain will actually throw themselves down and roll.

Repeated rolling can be a sign of colic.
▼

Colic Management

If your horse is rolling violently, stay out of his way. He won't know or care where he puts his feet or body. You could be hurt and you can't help him anyway, so stay clear.

If the horse looks uncomfortable but isn't in any way violent, it sometimes helps to put him on a long lead shank and walk him a bit, which can relieve a mild case of gas. However, walk him in an open area where you can easily get out of the way if he gets worse and goes down. Don't try to walk a horse that's in great discomfort; don't walk any horse to exhaustion.

In almost all cases of colic, it takes a veterinarian to know whether the problem is serious or not. Since colic can be so serious and, in fact, life threatening, never take the chance; if your horse looks like his belly hurts, and it lasts more than about 20 minutes, call the veterinarian immediately, even if the horse doesn't seem to be in a great deal of distress.

Never give your horse any pain medication before you talk to the veterinarian. The doctor needs to see firsthand how much pain the horse is in and how he responds to pain-relief medication.

Veterinary Exam for Colic

When the veterinarian comes, he or she will examine your horse, take his pulse, listen to his gut sounds, and probably perform a rectal examination. The veterinarian will then give the horse some pain medication, and maybe a sedative. He or she will watch the horse and tell you the suspected cause of the colic.

In some cases, the veterinarian will pass a tube through the horse's nose into his stomach to help determine if there's a big buildup of fluid or gas. Then, depending on what's found, the doctor may attach a pump to the free end of the tube and administer either water, mineral oil, or some other medication.

When the veterinarian thinks your horse is stable, he or she will leave you with specific instructions for watching the horse. Some horses have to be treated more than once before they get better. You may have to sleep in the barn to keep watch, but this will be worth it if it saves your horse.

In the worst cases of colic, the horse will need surgery. Great strides have been made in colic surgery and more horses are surviving than ever before, but it's still a risky procedure and an expensive one, even if you have equine medical facilities near you that routinely perform colic surgeries.

Some horses get through the surgery but not through the recovery period, or they develop adhesions in their intestines and colic again. When this happens there's not much point in going on. The horse likely will need to be euthanized.

Colic Causes

The absolute cause of all colic is unknown, but there are some things that make it more likely. If your horse doesn't have enough water available, or if he doesn't drink enough water because it's too dirty or cold, he may end up with dry, hard feces that can't pass down the intestine and become impacted. Some impactions can be resolved through medical treatment, while others require surgery.

It makes sense always to make absolutely sure your horse has plenty of clean water. If somebody else is responsible for watering, make it your business to double-check. Don't be rude, but do check, because it could save your horse's life. If your horse refuses to drink cold water in winter, you'll have to get him a bucket of slightly warmed water a couple of times a day. This is worth doing if it keeps your horse drinking, even though it can be time-consuming for you. An insulated water bucket may also help. Also make sure that automatic waterers are clean.

A second possible cause of colic is inadequate roughage. Roughage is good for the horse's gut: It keeps things moving. If the gut is empty, an intestinal twist can occur. To provide adequate roughage, make sure your horse has plenty of hay. Some horses are given alfalfa hay but only in small quantities, because it's so rich it can make some horses sick in larger amounts. But small amounts of alfalfa may not provide enough roughage, and your horse should still get good-quality grass hay.

A third likely factor in some colics is inadequate worming. Some types of worms common to horses migrate through the horse's intestines, or the blood vessels that supply the intestines. In passing, they can cause pieces of intestine or of the blood vessels to die. When this happens, the horse colics. Sometimes these cases can be fixed in surgery, and sometimes they can't. To prevent this problem, your horse always needs to be on a good worming program.

A sudden change of diet is yet another possible cause of colic. Don't switch grains suddenly; do it over a period of time. Try to feed pretty much the same kind of hay all the time.

Still, you should know that sometimes you can do all the right things and your horse will colic anyway. Be sure you know the signs of a sick horse, and call the veterinarian in early. Most veterinarians would much rather be called too soon than too late on a colic case. They'd also prefer to be called in the early evening than the middle of the night, so if your horse looks colicky at 5 P.M., call the veterinarian and ask if he or she wants to come out now, or to wait and see how things look a little later. Of course, if you find a horse in the middle of the night that has signs of colic, call the veterinarian immediately; don't wait until tomorrow. It could cost you your horse.

Diarrhea

Everybody knows what diarrhea is. In horses it can be very serious. If your horse has loose stool, watch him to make sure the problem doesn't get worse. Loose stool can be caused by eating rich green grass, a change in diet, or any of a number of other things, and usually it's nothing to worry about. But if your horse develops serious watery diarrhea, you need to call a veterinarian. Tell the doctor what you see and how long it has been going on. Diarrhea can dehydrate a horse quickly. In very serious cases, an otherwise healthy horse can die from untreated diarrhea in a day; foals can die even faster.

Furthermore, diarrhea may be due to an infectious disease that can spread to other horses. So if one horse in the barn gets a serious case of diarrhea, try to isolate him. Don't walk into another stall or touch another horse if you've been with the sick animal: Your shoes or hands could carry contaminants. Some contaminants can make people sick, too, so wash your hands carefully if you've been with a sick horse. Follow your veterinarian's directions.

Equine Protozoal Myelitis (EPM)

This is a neurologic disease many horsemen never heard of until fairly recently, but it's becoming increasingly common. EPM is caused by single-celled beings, called protozoans that set up housekeeping in a horse's spinal cord. Nobody is absolutely certain how horses become infected, but it's suspected that birds may be an intermediate host for the protozoans, and that opossums transmit the creatures to horses by contaminating hay, grain, water, or grass with their feces.

The disease occurs in all horse breeds. Because hay, grain, and horses are transported all over the country, and birds fly everywhere, EPM can be expected to turn up anywhere, although it's still found most often east of the Mississippi.

Health Records

Your horse will need to be seen regularly by a veterinarian for vaccinations and to have his teeth checked, and by the farrier to have his feet trimmed; you'll also need to worm him regularly. To make sure you don't skip important preventive health care, write it all down on a calendar that you use regularly. When one worming has been administered, write down when the next one is due.

In a separate file, keep bills from your veterinarian and farrier and any other health-related items. This way, they'll be there when you need to check the dates that care was administered.

A study under way at a major midwestern veterinary school indicates that almost 50 percent of horses, in a large random sample, have antibodies to the protozoans in their blood. These horses have been exposed to the protozoans that cause the disease. Nobody knows how many of the horses will ultimately show signs of the disease and, if they do, how long it will take for signs to appear. It could be 1 percent of them or less in 5 years or 10 years, or it could be a lot more. That research is still ongoing.

Signs of EPM

In the most typical case, a horse will show hind-end lameness that nobody can find a cause for. The lameness will be more pronounced on one side than the other, and there may be muscle wasting and weakness on that side. The horse may be slightly to moderately uncoordinated, especially in his back end. The hind-end lameness is actually a coordination problem, or a coordination problem that made the horse carry himself in an odd way until he became sore. However, many horses with EPM don't show these typical signs. Some have seizures, some develop generalized weakness, some have paralysis of the face, and some just act grumpy or demonstrate very bad behavior under saddle that isn't characteristic for them. This lack of standard clinical signs makes diagnosis of this disease difficult.

Testing for EPM

There's a blood test that can tell you if your horse has been exposed to EPM, but since 50 percent of the horses in some areas have been exposed, the test isn't all that helpful. A better blood test is in the works. For now, the only way to be sure of a diagnosis is for the horse to have a spinal tap. Ideally, any horse suspected of having EPM should be examined by a veterinarian experienced in performing neurologic exams and doing spinal taps. These are most likely to be found at large teaching hospitals or big clinics; some of these doctors are now doing several spinal taps a day.

EPM Treatment

As frightening as EPM is, the good news is that you can treat horses for it with good results. Of racehorses treated, about 65 percent recover well enough to return to racing. It can be presumed that an even higher percentage of pleasure horses will be able to return to their less demanding jobs successfully, especially if they're diagnosed and treated early on. The treatment involves administering oral drugs for at least 12 weeks. This in itself can be a headache, and it's extremely expensive — sometimes hundreds of dollars per month — but it can save your horse's life.

Expect new information about this disease to come forth often. However, whenever you do hear new things about EPM, be sure to check the source: Misinformation is coming forth much faster than the real thing.

Eye Problems

Any eye problem in a horse requires the attention of a veterinarian. Such problems can worsen quickly, and could cost your horse his sight.

One type of eye problem is due to injury, which can result in a corneal ulcer and complications if not treated promptly and properly. Antibiotics may well be prescribed, but great care must be taken never to put eye products containing steroids in the eye of a horse with a corneal ulcer. It can result in loss of the eye.

Horses can also develop various types of eye diseases. One is night blindness. A horse that can't see in the dark might shy or behave oddly when moving from a lighted to a dark area. Horses with night blindness don't get worse with age — they're as badly affected as foals as they are as adults. In milder cases, it's probably something you can live with, as long as you know what's going on.

Moon blindness, also called uveitis, is another potential eye problem. With this disease, the horse suffers bouts of painful eye inflammation that can cause watering and squinting. Sometimes ulcers develop on the eye. This condition can get worse with time and lead to blindness in one or both eyes. Medical treatment can alleviate much of the discomfort and slow the progress of the disease in many horses.

Other eye problems that horses can develop include cataracts and abnormalities of the retina.

Heatstroke

You must take care in hot weather to keep your horse from getting overheated, which can lead to heatstroke. In hot weather, then, don't overdo the exercise, especially if it's humid, too, which makes it harder for the horse to cool down. A horse that's overheated may act weak, stop eating, or, in more serious cases, collapse and even die.

On those hot summer days, try to ride early in the morning or in the evening when the temperature isn't so high. Take care to give your horse relief if he becomes hot by hosing him down. If you suspect a problem, take the horse's temperature. If it is above 102°F, hose him with cold water. If the temperature stays elevated, call your veterinarian.

If his stall gets hot in summer months, provide a fan to keep the air moving.

Hyperkalemic Periodic Paralysis (HYPP)

This is a genetic defect that may occur in Quarter Horses, and less often in Appaloosas and Paints. If a horse has the defect, you can't tell by looking. The problem is that the metabolism of his cells does not function correctly, particularly regarding calcium transmission. This can lead to tremors, mild to severe seizures, or even sudden collapse and death. If diagnosed, the horse can sometimes be helped with dietary adjustments and medication, but sometimes he can't be helped.

The disease can be traced back to one sire in the Quarter Horse breed named Impressive. Impressive was a truly great halter horse, and a great breeding sire. His name is estimated to appear somewhere on about 40 percent of the pedigrees of living Quarter Horses. He was also used as a sire of Paints and Appaloosas. Unfortunately, he passed on this serious genetic defect to some of his offspring.

Blood Testing

It took a long time for anybody to figure all of this out, so Impressive's offspring themselves became the sires and dams of many horses, and the gene, which it turns out is a dominant gene, was passed on to many more horses. Now that the genetics of this defect are understood, a blood test can be done that will enable your veterinarian to tell you if your horse is affected. Even if a horse has this genetic defect, though, it's not always possible to know whether he'll have problems as a result or not. However, horses who inherited the gene from both the sire's and the dam's families are almost sure to have problems.

In the meantime, there's a sort of Oklahoma-land-rush-in-reverse going on to sell off horses related to Impressive to the unsuspecting. Some are being sold without being tested for this genetic defect, and sometimes you can snag an unaffected horse for a great price. Others being sold are affected but the seller isn't about to mention it.

The bottom line on all this is: Buyer beware. If someone tells you that a Quarter Horse for sale isn't affected, don't just take the seller's word. Ask to see the documentation, or make the sale contingent on testing. Have your own veterinarian handle this.

The good news is that once everybody stops breeding HYPP-positive horses, the problem will disappear, and the remaining, unaffected sires and dams from the Impressive line could go on to produce top-quality animals.

Laminitis and Founder

Laminitis and founder are serious conditions. The two words are often used interchangeably, but they actually refer to separate conditions. Laminitis involves an inflammation of the laminae, which are sensitive tissues in the horse's feet. If it progresses, a bone in the bottom of the foot known as the coffin bone actually rotates, and this is called founder.

Signs of Laminitis

A horse with laminitis will have sore feet. If you notice that your horse doesn't seem to feel good and he also seems extremely unwilling to walk, even out of his stall, it could be laminitis. Sometimes horses with laminitis will stand with their hind legs tucked underneath the body. This happens because laminitis most often affects the front feet: The horse is trying to take weight off the painful areas by supporting as much of himself as he can with his back feet. In some cases, laminitis and founder can also affect the rear feet.

If you suspect a horse has laminitis, call a veterinarian immediately. If the condition is allowed to progress, the laminae break down and the resulting founder can be so bad that the coffin bone can actually come through the bottom of the sole. A horse suffering this bad a case may well have to be destroyed.

In less serious cases the horse may be saved, but this often requires a long, painful recovery and sometimes surgery. In the mildest cases, the horse may need to wear special shoes, or may be minimally affected. How it all comes out may depend on how fast you get a veterinarian out to treat your horse.

Causes of Laminitis

A number of things can lead to laminitis and founder. One is overeating grain. Another is too much rich pasture, which generally occurs in the spring when the grass is rich, especially if the horse isn't used to being on pasture. Horses not used to grass should be put out for 15 minutes at first; this time should be increased day by day until he can accommodate the time you want to allow him outside.

Ponies and cresty-necked horses, such as some Morgans, are thought to be more prone to laminitis and founder, but any breed of horse can develop these problems. Nobody is absolutely sure why. Just be especially careful with ponies and cresty-necked horses.

Some medications, especially steroids, may have the side effect of causing laminitis, which is why all medications should be used only under the advice of a veterinarian.

Another type of founder, road founder, is caused by concussion to the feet. This can happen if the horse is used fast and hard on solid surfaces, such as roads. It can also happen if the horse is worked unusually hard just after a big change in shoeing. For example, a horse that has always gone barefoot but is shod to attend a big fair or show and then worked especially hard at the show can road-founder. A horse that has always worn shoes, has them pulled, and is then worked hard can road-founder.

Navicular Disease

The navicular bone is a smooth little pyramid-shaped bone that lies deep in the center of the foot. Its purpose is to act as a sort of pulley for a tendon. When the horse has navicular disease, this little navicular bone becomes rough, and the tendon fails to slide over it smoothly. This causes the horse pain. Nobody is sure of the cause of navicular disease; there may be some genetic component.

The worst aspects of navicular disease are that it gets worse over time and there is no cure. In its early stages, the discomfort to the horse can be eased with pain relievers. He may be helped by special shoeing or other medication. Eventually, however, the horse can become unusable.

Navicular disease seems to be more common in heavy-bodied horses with small feet, which is the way some Quarter Horses are bred, as well as some Appaloosas and Paints. In these breeds, it also seems to be more common among animals that have been halter horses that were kept quite fat from an early age and didn't get much work. It also crops up in some horses that have been used at hard work such as jumping, and in some horses for no reason that anyone can name.

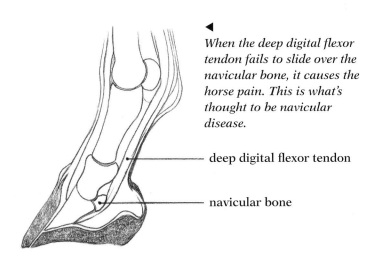

◀

When the deep digital flexor tendon fails to slide over the navicular bone, it causes the horse pain. This is what's thought to be navicular disease.

deep digital flexor tendon

navicular bone

Sole Abscess

A sole abscess is a pocket of infection in the sole of the horse's foot. It sometimes happens after the foot has been bruised, and sometimes to horses that have foundered in the past. It can also happen because the feet are not well maintained and serious deep cracks have formed that allow dirt into the soft tissues inside the foot. And it can happen for no obvious reason.

A sole abscess is very painful. Often the horse will look fine one day and be three-legged lame the next. Sometimes, he'll lie down for long periods to get the weight off his foot. If you've ever had an abscessed tooth, you'll have a clue how painful an abscess can be to a horse, and have mercy!

If you suspect an abscess, call the veterinarian or your farrier, who will open up a hole in the sole of the foot to allow the infection to drain out. You may be instructed to soak the foot in warm water and Epsom salts a couple of times a day, and you'll have to keep the hole bandaged for a time to prevent more dirt from getting up into the foot.

Some veterinarians may elect to put a horse with an abscess on antibiotics. They may also advise packing the foot with a substance that will help draw the infection out of it.

In classic cases of abscess of the foot, the moment the infection is allowed to drain out, the horse feels better.

Strangles

Strangles is an infectious disease that typically causes the lymph glands between a horse's jaws to swell with infection. Usually an abscess forms between his jaws, which eventually drains. In most cases, the horse will act like he doesn't feel good. He may have a discharge from his nostrils and an elevated temperature. The swelling in the lymph nodes between the jaws usually appears a couple of days after the first signs of illness. The horse will begin to get better after the abscess has come to a head and drained.

If you see a swelling, talk to your veterinarian about how to best manage the disease. Administering antibiotics to a horse that currently has abcesses can result in recurrent abcesses all over the body. This condition is properly called *bastard strangles,* and it can be very serious.

Do keep the horse isolated, because strangles is very contagious. The organism that causes the disease can be spread among horses drinking from the same water trough, or it can be carried on your hands or shoes from one horse to another. Wash your hands well before you touch any other horses. Change your shoes before you go in with other horses, then disinfect the first shoes.

There is a strangles vaccine. Some veterinarians seem to think highly of it; others don't. Talk with your own veterinarian to make the best decision for your horse.

Thrush

Thrush is a fungal infection of the foot that has a characteristically foul odor. It causes a black, tarry substance. Thrush is most likely to occur in damp, unclean conditions. Thrush can seriously damage a horse's foot if left untreated, and can lead to lameness.

To prevent thrush, keep your horse's feet clean, and his stall clean and dry. If he develops a case of smelly feet, there are several thrush preparations on the market that can be used to treat it or you can use chlorine bleach. If the problem doesn't clear up in a few days, contact your farrier for help.

▲
Keeping the feet clean by regular picking will help prevent thrush.

Tying Up

The medical term for this condition was formerly azoturia; today, it's usually called *exertional rhabdomyelosis*. It's not fully understood. There may be a genetic component to some types of this illness; in other types no one knows the cause. When it happens, the muscles — especially the large muscles of the rump — become rigid and hard. This causes the horse considerable pain. He walks with very short steps, if he walks at all. In addition, the horse may sweat or may have a rapid pulse due to pain. Often the urine will be dark, even coffee colored.

Tying up used to be called *Monday morning disease,* because it often happened to draft horses that were given Sunday off and then went back to plowing on Monday. Today, Monday incidence is still seen in Amish work horses. It seems to happen less if the horse's grain ration is reduced on the days he is not worked.

Tying up is also seen in horses, such as race and event horses, that do fast hard work. It's sometimes seen in horses that are worked hard at a show and then trailered home.

If after hard work your horse acts as though he doesn't want to move, especially if his rump muscles seem very hard, let him be. Don't try to make him walk, and call the veterinarian. The veterinarian may administer pain medication and intravenous fluids.

You can minimize the risk of tying up by keeping your horse on a regular exercise program and feeding schedule; when you aren't working him as much, reduce the amount of grain you give him.

Wound Care

If a horse has a very minor scrape or wound that looks clean, applying some antibiotic ointment is probably sufficient treatment. A minor wound that looks dirty can be rinsed with clean water, then further cleaned with soap or a surgical scrub; an antiseptic lotion or ointment can then be applied.

Anything other than a minor wound should be checked out by a veterinarian. Certainly you should apply pressure to stop bleeding, if necessary, but other than this, don't apply any products unless your veterinarian tells you to while you wait for him or her to arrive.

Unless you are positive that your horse has had a tetanus vaccination recently, it is advisable to administer another one after a horse sustains any wound that's dirty or deep, such as a puncture wound. Be sure to ask your veterinarian about this.

Routine Treatments and Tests

Just like people, your horse needs routine maintenance to stay healthy. His teeth need some care, he needs to be vaccinated against a variety of infectious diseases, and he needs to be wormed regularly. He may need to be tranquilized for some procedures and, at some time in his life, he may need pain medication. Familiarize yourself with these routine treatments.

Coggins Test

A Coggins test is a blood test for equine infectious anemia (EIA). EIA is a nasty disease that's contagious to horses through the bites of contaminated insects, but for which there's no cure. So a horse with EIA can be bitten by a fly, which then bites another horse and transmits the disease. The disease itself may or may not be fatal to the horse, but in either case, the infected animal is a reservoir of EIA just waiting for an insect to carry it to another horse.

EIA is actually uncommon today, but it's such a serious disease that strict controls are kept in place to ensure it doesn't spread. Consequently, the federal government and most state governments require that all shipped horses be tested. Horses that have positive Coggins tests must be destroyed or permanently quarantined.

Most states require arriving horses to have had a Coggins test done no more than one year before they enter the state. Many horse shows require a current Coggins — one performed within the past year. (Some require one within six months; check the rules.) Most horsepeople who show or haul to trail rides out of state have a Coggins done every year along with each horse's routine vaccinations.

Before you buy any horse, make sure he has a current negative Coggins. Watch out at auctions in particular. It's common for blood to be drawn for a Coggins test at the auction. The new owner then gets the results a couple of weeks later. In the rare cases in which the test is positive, it's the buyer of the horse who's out his or her money and the horse. The logic is that the buyer knew the horse was being tested at the sale, and therefore knowingly assumed the risk. *Caveat emptor!* ("Let the buyer beware.")

When you get Coggins results, you receive an official piece of paper that includes the name of the horse, a description and drawing of his markings, the date the test was run, and the signature of the veterinarian who drew the sample. The paper is issued by a state laboratory. It may take a couple of weeks or more for the paper to get to you after the test is run. If you need a Coggins for a show, then, be sure to allow plenty of time for your veterinarian to draw the sample, send it to the state lab to be processed, and send the results to you.

Floating Teeth

Floating means "making level." To float a horse's teeth, then, means to level them, just as you float concrete to level it off. In horses, this is accomplished with a tool called a dental float.

Horses require floating because their teeth can develop rough edges. When they chew, they move their jaws from side to side. The molars (the teeth in the back of the mouth) are used for grinding. As a horse ages and eats, the grinding wears away parts of his teeth and tends to leave sharp edges on the outsides. These sharp edges can jab the horse in the inside of the cheeks, especially when a bridle is used. Sometimes the horse wears his teeth down in such a way that it's almost impossible for him to eat normally.

Signs of Tooth Trouble

Tooth trouble can cause a variety of problems in horses ranging from discomfort to weight loss. Signs that your horse needs dental attention include:

✓ Trouble chewing, such as holding the head sideways while eating or apparent discomfort while eating

✓ Dropping feed out of the mouth while eating

✓ Whole pieces of grain in the manure

✓ Avoidance of the bit in a horse that previously accepted it

✓ Weight loss

✓ Facial swelling near the teeth

For these reasons, you must have your horse's teeth looked after on a routine basis. The veterinarian, or horse dentist, will usually hold the horse's mouth open with a device called a mouth speculum, and then file off the rough edges with the dental float.

Your horse should have his teeth examined when he gets his routine vaccinations. But if at any time you notice that he seems to have trouble chewing, there are whole pieces of grain in his manure, or he's dropping a lot of feed as he eats, it's probably time to have his teeth floated.

If your horse has always been a calm animal but suddenly seems to react violently when you touch him with the bit, perhaps rearing, he may have a sore tooth that needs dental attention.

Hoof Care

Horses need to have their hooves trimmed regularly to keep them in balance. Most horses that are ridden also need shoes to protect their feet.

A farrier can provide this service, which will need to be done anywhere from every four weeks in warm weather, when hooves grow faster, to every eight weeks in cold winter months.

To find a good farrier, ask several other horse owners and see which farrier's name comes up the most. If you board your horse at a barn, the barn may have one farrier it uses routinely.

Stool Check

Have your horse's stool checked for parasites once or twice yearly, as your veterinarian recommends. A sample can be taken during routine visits for vaccinations. A stool check is a good way to tell if your worming program (see below) is working.

Worming

Keeping horses on a routine worming program is crucial to preventing colic and other medical problems. Worming is easy, because the products come in a paste form that's readily administered from a tube. All you have to do is squirt the paste well into your horse's mouth. Your veterinarian can tell you what products to use, and when to use them, which will vary depending on your horse's living conditions.

Many equine veterinarians, however, agree that horses should be wormed with a good product about every eight weeks. The worming products you use need to be rotated, because parasites can build up a resistance to some wormers.

Also, some products don't work on all parasites, or all life forms of a parasite. Botflies, for example, are resistant to some common worming products. Some wormers can be used on foals; others can't. Some can be used on pregnant mares; others can't. Furthermore, worming products change from time to time. For all these reasons, it's wise to let your veterinarian be your guide through the maze of products and worming schedules.

Some horsemen use a daily wormer called pyrantel tartrate (Strongid), which is administered in the feed. It's considered an adequate product and is supposed to reduce parasite-associated colic. It doesn't kill bots, however, so horses on this product still require periodic worming with another product effective against bots, as recommended by your veterinarian. Some parasites can develop resistance to this product, so you need to do periodic fecal exams to determine its effectiveness.

Vaccinations

Your horse will need a variety of annual vaccinations. Which ones he gets will vary somewhat depending on the part of the United States in which you live. Let your veterinarian tell you what you need. Here are some of the most common vaccinations.

Tetanus

All horses need a tetanus shot every year. Tetanus is an awful disease that's almost always fatal. It's rarely seen these days, though, because all horsemen vaccinate against it. The vaccination is extremely cheap insurance, so make sure you do it every year. Most veterinarians recommend an extra tetanus shot if a horse gets a deep cut between his annual vaccinations.

Encephalomyelitis

Sleeping sickness is the common name for another ugly disease that horses can get from insects. The medical name is encephalomyelitis, and there's more than one form of it. For this reason, most horses are vaccinated against both the eastern and western varieties of the disease, and often the Venezuelan. Some states require vaccinations for any horse within their borders or entering the state.

Rhinopneumonitis

Rhinopneumonitis is a disease that you can usually avoid by vaccination. Rhino, as it's called, is sometimes serious in itself, and causes symptoms like those of a person with a very bad cold. It's also highly contagious, however, and can cause pregnant mares to abort their foals.

Horses with rhino need lots of rest and TLC, may be out of work for days, and even then won't be up to peak performance. For these reasons, most horsemen vaccinate against it. Pregnant mares need a series of rhino vaccinations, usually at 3, 5, 7, and 9 months of pregnancy to prevent abortion.

Influenza

If you show your horse or take him often to places where there are other horses, you'll need to vaccinate for flu about every two months. This may seem like a lot of trouble and expense, but you'll find it's cheaper and easier than having a horse get sick exactly when you want to ride him most.

Rabies

Many people are surprised to learn that horses can get rabies. It doesn't happen often, but of course when it does the horse always dies a horrible death. If your horse gets rabies, you'll need to get rabies shots yourself. Depending on where you live, and how your horse is kept, you might consider an annual rabies vaccination for him. Horses that spend a great deal of time outside in pasture in areas where rabies is found are the most susceptible to it. Usually the horse contracts the disease from an infected skunk, fox, or raccoon that's wandering through the pasture. The sick animal looks peculiar, the horse curiously puts his nose down to investigate, and gets bitten. Ask your veterinarian if you should vaccinate against rabies.

Other diseases that may require vaccinations crop up in specific parts of the United States. As veterinary research continues, vaccinations for new diseases or new varieties of old diseases may be developed. For this reason you need to ask your veterinarian what shots should be given each year.

Tranquilizers

There are times when it's reasonable to administer a tranquilizer to a horse. Horses that don't trailer well and must be transported, for example, may benefit from a tranquilizer. You really shouldn't tranquilize your horse yourself: Call your veterinarian. But in the real world, many horse barns have tranquilizers on hand, so you ought to know what they are, how they're used, and what can go wrong.

Acetylpromazine (Acepromazine)

This common injectable product is often referred to as "ace." Given as an injection in the muscle, it takes effect in about 15 to 20 minutes, and will last a couple of hours.

What's important to know is that the response to ace can vary widely among horses. Just a little will tranquilize some animals nearly to oblivion, while for others a great deal won't do much at all. This is why your veterinarian needs to decide how much to administer.

If you're planning to haul a horse on ace, remember that he may be more tranquil, but he'll also be less coordinated and less stable on his feet.

Ace should never be used on a horse that's already excited. It very likely will make him wilder.

Xylazine (Rompun)

A slightly less common drug around horse barns is xylazine (Rompun). This is an injectable that, if given in the muscle, requires about 15 minutes to take effect, and lasts 15 to 30 minutes more. Xylazine is sometimes used to calm down horses that are already distressed. Be forewarned that if a horse has been given xylazine, you should avoid his back end. More than a few horses on this drug will kick fast and hard for apparently no reason, even though they look sedate and tranquil. This can happen with horses that don't kick at all when they aren't tranquilized.

Pain Medication

Medication is often the most effective way to manage a horse's pain. Consult your veterinarian if you suspect use of pain medication is warranted.

Phenylbutazone

"Bute," as it's often called, is the most common pain medication for horses. It's a nonsteroidal, anti-inflammatory product.

As with all drugs, it can be very helpful if used wisely. On the one hand, you don't want your horse on drugs if he doesn't need them; on the other, if your veterinarian says he needs bute, give it to him. You're probably doing him a kindness, and you can rest assured that he won't become an addict.

Be aware that there are rules about how much bute a horse can have in his bloodstream at shows. The American Quarter Horse Association doesn't allow any. The American Horse Show Association does allow it, but only at specific levels.

Do not, under any circumstances, take phenylbutazone yourself. Some people think it's like taking an aspirin, but it's not. Bute is sometimes prescribed for people, but a physician must monitor the patient because the drug can cause a condition called aplastic anemia, which is fatal. Every year, it seems that a few jockeys or rodeo riders or horsepeople become stiff and sore, take the bute they keep for their horses — and sometimes die.

> ### Injection Warning
>
> Never let anybody other than your veterinarian give a horse an injection into a vein. This process can look easy to some people, so they try it. If they don't know what they're doing and put medication into an artery instead of a vein, they can kill the horse.

Appendixes

A: Feeding Your Horse

EQUINE NUTRITION IS A GIGANTIC, COMPLEX SUBJECT. Nobody comes close to knowing it all, even after years of study and advanced degrees. Still, you need to have some idea of what to feed your horse. In the United States, most people feed some sort of hay and some sort of grain.

Forage

Horses are designed to be foragers. They're built to slowly munch their way through life rather than eat one or two huge meals daily. Horse intestines need to have food passing down the pipeline nearly all the time, or a number of things can go wrong. The worst of these things is that the intestines might twist, which means colic (although a horse with a full gut might also develop a twisted intestine). For this reason alone it makes sense to feed your horse in such a way that her intestines get to work the way they were meant to. This means that she should have access to pasture or hay most of the time.

Of course, if your horse has access to hay or pasture all day and all night, she can end up with well-functioning intestines and a big weight problem if she isn't exercised enough. To avoid this you could limit her access to the hay or pasture, or you could increase the amount of work she's doing to burn off some of those calories.

Hay

Hay is grass or other plants, such as clover or alfalfa, that's cut and dried for food. Not all hays are the same; one type can be very different from another.

Grass Hays

Grass hays, a common source of roughage for horses, include timothy, orchard grass, bermuda grass, fescue, and bromegrass. Generally, they're not high in protein; it takes a reasonably large quantity of grass hay to provide a horse with her nutritional requirements for a day. This means

Feed Changes

Changes in feeding have been associated with an increased risk for colic. So if you change your horse's diet, do it gradually.

Good horsemen are even careful not to make an abrupt change from grass hay to a legume hay such as alfalfa. It's possible, though not probable, that such a sudden change could result in colic.

◄ *Horses are foragers. They benefit from ready access to pasture and hay.*

you have to wrestle with a bunch of hay every day to feed your horse, but a large quantity of hay is just what her guts are built to handle.

The only way you can find out for sure whether she's getting what she needs from her hay is to have the hay tested. Your county Agricultural Extension Agent or the representatives of most feed companies can tell you how to have this done. It's not ruinously expensive and the information is quite useful. Beware of fescue: It can carry a fungus that can cause serious problems for pregnant mares. Fescue should only be used for horses if it is certified "endophyte free," or free of the fungus.

Beware Moldy Hay

Horses need to eat good-quality, clean hay. If the hay smells slightly moldy, looks dark, or seems to have little white specks of mold on it, throw it away. Horses won't eat moldy hay if they have a choice, but if they do, it can lead to fatal mold poisoning. Don't take a chance. Call your supplier and have the moldy bales replaced.

Cattle, by the way, can digest hay that horses can't tolerate. Don't assume that hay being fed to cattle is safe for horses.

Alfalfa

The second major type of hay you're likely to run into is alfalfa hay. Alfalfa is a legume and higher in protein than grass hay. High-quality alfalfa hay sometimes looks so good you want to try it yourself, and horses love the stuff.

But alfalfa can really put the pounds on your horse. Some of it is so rich that the only way to control your horse's weight is to severely limit the amount of hay she gets. This may mean she feels hungry, even if her weight looks about right to you. And a horse that feels hungry or has a deep desire to munch something after her hay is consumed may just go ahead and eat your fences or your barn. If her guts are unhappy, she could colic as well.

In addition, some horses can't tolerate alfalfa hay, because it's just too rich. A horse that has ever had laminitis or foundered should not be fed alfalfa, which could cause her to founder again.

To make life more complicated, the ratio of calcium to phosphorus in a horse's diet is crucial. Some alfalfa hay is so rich in calcium that it can upset this balance, which will throw a whole bunch of other metabolic requirements out of whack. This could mean serious health problems for your horse at some point. That point will probably arrive sooner in young growing horses and mares in foal, but you never know when it might come. I recommend you thus have your alfalfa hay tested for nutritional components, just so you know what you've got, then balance the rest of the feed ration accordingly.

Mixed Hays

Many horse owners feed mixed hays. These are likely to include alfalfa; clover, which is a legume like alfalfa; and grass. Such mixtures work well for most horses. (Note that clover hay can be dusty.)

Managing Hay

Try to find one good steady source of hay. If you don't you'll be at the mercy of hay farmers, and so will your horse, because you'll change her nutrition with each load of hay you bring in. If you switch from alfalfa to timothy, for instance, at the drop of a hat, you could end up with a sick horse. So if you've been feeding timothy, try to stick with it.

Hay can be difficult to handle if you don't have your place set up to facilitate moving and storing it. Baled hay is heavy, and it must be stored properly so it doesn't mold and make horses sick. Some horse owners, in fact, find it so much trouble to handle hay that they try to make do with little of it, feeding more grains to keep weight on their horses. But horses need the roughage they get from hay. In addition, grain costs much more than hay ounce per ounce. If handling hay is proving to be a problem for you, a better solution might be to use hay cubes as part of the hay ration (described below).

Feeding Hay Amounts

A general rule is to provide your horse with at least 2 pounds of good hay per 100 pounds of live weight daily. A 1,000-pound horse, then, needs about 20 pounds of hay each day.

If you're feeding grass hay, you can give your horse continuous access to this roughage as long as she's not getting overweight and you can afford to provide this much.

Winter Feeding

Hay helps horses keep warm, because the process of digesting it generates heat. In winter, you may want to feed your horse more hay to help fight the cold.

Hay Cubes

Hay cubes come in bags, and are easier to handle than bales. They have another advantage, too: they're consistent. If you buy the same type from the same manufacturer, you won't be changing your horse's nutrition with each new bag. But hay cubes do vary markedly in quality from one manufacturer to another.

Be careful how you introduce hay cubes into the diet. Don't just switch from bales to cubes one day: Instead, follow the feed company's recommendations about how much to feed. Hay cubes are digested efficiently. It is essential that cubes be fed at least three times per day; less frequent feeding may easily cause colic.

Hay cubes aren't cheap, and some horses feel so "chew deprived" after they eat their cubes that they may even attack the woodwork. If you switch to cubes, do so slowly and observe your horse carefully to see how she's faring. Hay cubes are a good choice for horses with a breathing problem.

▲
If managing bales of hay is a problem, consider using hay cubes as part of the hay ration.

Grain

Grain of some sort, usually oats, corn, or a blend of grains in the form of manufactured pellets, is the other component of most U.S. horse diets. The truth is that many adult horses can get along fine without any grain at all, just good-quality hay. (This is not a good idea for young horses or pregnant mares.) But Americans like to make themselves feel good and put a smile on their horses' faces by giving them some grain. If you're trying to achieve a balanced diet for your horse, as you should, the grain she eats should be selected to complement her hay.

If your horse is eating calcium-rich alfalfa hay, for instance, her grain should be different from that of a horse eating grass hay. This means you really need to have a conversation with a feed company representative before you decide what to feed your horse.

Many people give "sweet feed," which is grain often mixed with pellets (in England pellets are called "pony nuts") and held together with molasses to keep the dust down and make the feed tasty for horses. Horses like sweet feed, and from their point of view, the sweeter the better.

Not all sweet feed is the same; its quality depends on the manufacturer. Some manufacturers use protein in the feed from any number of different places, and it can change from one load to the next. These tend to be cheaper feeds.

Good feed companies use consistent sources of protein, and sources that are useful for horses. Buy from reputable companies. Don't just look for the cheapest feed. The best companies will have people knowledgeable in horse nutrition that you can talk to. If you haven't a clue which feed product to use, ask a veterinarian or two for some recommendations.

Feeding Grain Amounts

How much grain to feed your horse depends on what type of horse you have and what sort of work she's doing. Start by asking her previous owner what she was getting; if she's in good condition, continue with that amount. If your horse is overweight, though, you might want to cut back a bit on her grain; if she needs to gain a few pounds, you can add a bit. Always make changes gradually, over the course of several days.

When providing grain, serve two or three small portions daily rather than giving it all at once: This is crucial to avoid digestive problems and illness.

Weighing Feed

When it comes to feeding your horse be aware that weight and volume differ. It's an elementary concept, of course, but it's also important. A 5-pound coffee can, for example, came into this world to hold 5 pounds of coffee — a unit of weight. If you dumped the coffee out, filled the can to the top with feathers, and weighed it, it would come in at well less than 5 pounds.

Different horse grains weigh different amounts. If you fill the can with sweet feed it might weigh 5 pounds, and it might not. The same is true of oats. If one horse in your barn is getting a coffee can full of sweet feed and her neighbor is getting the same can full of oats, you can't presume they're both getting 5 pounds of feed. In this case, you're using the can as a measure of volume, not weight.

This is important because your veterinarian or feed company representative may work out a good diet for your horse that tells you

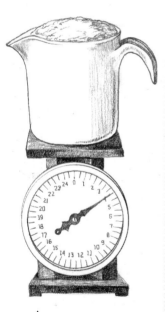

▲
Feed should be weighed, not served by volume.

how much grain to feed in pounds. If you're using the coffee can to measure rather than weigh the feed, you may not be giving your horse what you think you are. It's better to weigh the feed.

Water

Ready access to water is crucial to your horse's well-being. The average adult horse will drink anywhere from 8 to 10 gallons of water daily, and more if she's been working hard. So make sure your horse has a continual supply of fresh water.

If she's stalled you must check her water bucket three or four times a day, unless you have an automatic waterer. If you can't check the water this often, then you need at least two buckets. If you have an automatic waterer, check it routinely to make sure it's working and clean.

In the winter, it's imperative that your horse's water doesn't get so cold that she won't drink it or that it freezes over, making it impossible for her to drink. Under such conditions, ice in the buckets must be broken up and removed, and warm water should be provided to the horse at least twice daily, preferably more. Some horses don't like cold water. If you use buckets, keep a rough tally of how much the horse is drinking. You may have to provide warm water to encourage the horse to drink enough.

If your horse lives outdoors and drinks from a water tub, the tub should be kept clean. In winter, an insulated bucket to keep the water from freezing is a good idea. If your horse drinks from a stream, make sure it hasn't frozen over.

Salt

Horses need salt. It's as vital to their well-being as hay and water. If they don't get enough salt, they'll develop a poor appetite and can lose weight and condition.

To ensure that your horse has adequate salt, provide her with a salt block at all times, winter and summer. Many veterinarians prefer you use a mineralized salt block, which provides minerals that may be inadequate in some forages.

Supplements

Start reading the ads for dietary supplements in horse magazines and you may become convinced your horse needs most of them. But the philosophy that "more is better" just isn't true when it comes to adding things to your horse's diet.

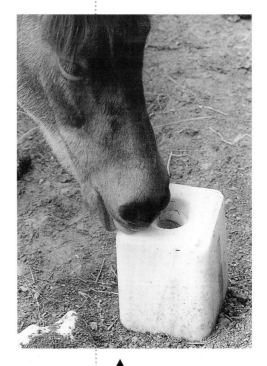

▲
Salt is important for horses. They should have access to a salt or mineralized salt block all year long.

The moment you start adding supplements to a balanced diet, you have unbalanced the diet. Simply chucking things into your horse's meals as a "bonus" could really cause you problems. This is especially true of young and growing horses.

Ask your veterinarian what, if anything, you need to supplement and how best to do so. Some parts of the United States are deficient in certain minerals and a supplement may well be in order, but in other areas, you may just be throwing money away or even doing harm to your horse by supplementing. Certain conditions in horses, such as poor hair coats and weak hooves, may also benefit from a supplement, but ask your veterinarian before you spend your money.

B: Horse Associations

American Connemara
  Pony Society
32600 Fairmount Boulevard
Pepper Pike, OH 44124

American Hackney Horse
  Society
4059 Iron Works Pike
Lexington, KY 40511
606-255-8694

American Hanoverian
  Horse Society
4059 Iron Works Pike, Bldg. C
Lexington, KY 40511
606-255-4141

American Holsteiner Horse
  Association, Inc.
222 East Main Street, Suite 1
Georgetown, KY 40324
502-863-4239

American Miniature Horse
  Association
5601 South Interstate 35 West
Alvarado, TX 76009
817-783-5600

American Miniature Horse
  Registry
6748 N. Frostwood Parkway
Peoria, IL 61615
309-691-9671

American Morgan Horse
  Association
P.O. Box 960
Shelburne, VT 05482
802-985-4944

American Paint Horse
  Association
P.O. Box 961023
Fort Worth, TX 76101
817-439-3400

American Quarter Horse
  Association
P.O. Box 200
Amarillo, TX 79168
806-376-4811

American Saddlebred Horse
  Association
4093 Iron Works Pike
Lexington, KY 40511
606-259-2742

American Shetland Pony Club
81B Queenwood
Morton, IL 61550
309-263-4044

American Trakehner
  Association
1520 West Church Street
Newark, OH 43055
740-344-1111

Appaloosa Horse Club
5070 Highway 8 West
Moscow, ID 83843
208-882-5578

California Miniature Trotting
  Association
8340 Bianchi Road
Roseville, CA 95747
1-800-NOW-MINI

Friesian Horse Association
  of North America
P.O. Box 1809
Sisters, OR 97759
541-549-4272

Haflinger Association of America
14570 Gratiot Road
Hemlock, MI 48626
517-642-5307

Haflinger Breeders
    Organization, Inc.
85 South Street
Rockport, MA 01966
978-546-3748

Haflinger Registry of North
    America
14640 S.R. 83
Coshocton, OH 43812
614-829-2790

International Arabian Horse
    Association
10805 East Bethany Drive
Aurora, CO 80014
303-696-4500

International Quarter Pony
    Association
P.O. Box 125
Sheridan, CA 95681
916-645-9313

The Jockey Club
    (Thoroughbreds)
821 Corporate Drive
Lexington, KY 40503
606-224-2700

Masters of Foxhounds
    Association
Morven Park, P.O. Box 2420
Leesburg, VA 20177
703-771-7442

Missouri Fox Trotting Horse
    Breed Association
P.O. Box 1027
Ava, MO 65608
417-683-2468

National Mustang Association
P.O. Box 1367
Cedar City, UT 84721-1367
888-867-8662

National Show Horse Registry
11700 Commonwealth Drive
Louisville, KY 40299
502-266-5100

NA/WPN Dutch Warmblood
P.O. Box 0
Sutherlin, OR 97497
541-459-3232

North American Trakehner
    Association
P.O. Box 12172
Lexington, KY 40581
502-867-0375

Palomino Horse Breeders
    Association of America, Inc.
15243 East Skelly Drive
Tulsa, OK 74116-2637
918-438-1234

Paso Fino Horse Association,
    Inc.
101 North Collins Street
Plant City, FL 33566-3311
813-719-7777

Performance Horse Registry
P.O. 24710
Lexington, KY 40525-4710
800-787-0027

Peruvian Paso Horse Registry
3077 Wiljan Court, Suite A
Santa Rosa, CA 95407
707-579-4394

Pinto Horse Association of
    America
1900 Samuels Avenue
Fort Worth, TX 76102-1141
817-336-7842

Pony of the Americas Club, Inc.
5240 Elmwood Avenue
Indianapolis, IN 46203
317-788-0107

The Racking Horse Breeders
    Association of America
Route 2, Box 72-A
Decatur, AL 35603
205-353-7225

Rocky Mountain Horse
    Association
6569 East Highway 36
Olympia, KY 40358
606-674-2859

Tennessee Walking Horse
    Breeders' and Exhibitors'
    Association
P.O. Box 286
Lewisburg, TN 37091
800-359-1574

United States Dressage
    Federation
P.O. Box 6669
Lincoln, NE 68506-0669
402-434-8550

United States Icelandic Horse
    Congress
38 Park Street
Montclair, NJ 07042
973-783-3429

United States Trotting Associa-
    tion (Standardbreds)
750 Michigan Avenue
Columbus, OH 43215
614-224-2291

C: Recommended Reading

Books

Barns, Sheds & Outbuildings: Placement, Design and Construction, by Byron D. Halstead (Alan C. Hood, Chambersburg, PA, 1995).

A Companion Guide to Riding Lessons, by Michael W. Smith (Storey Books, Pownal, VT, 1998). Learn how to ride correctly and have fun doing it. Smith also features a horse in each chapter.

Complete Plans for Building Horse Barns Big and Small, 2nd ed., by Nancy W. Ambrosiano and Mary F. Harcourt (Breakthrough Publications, Ossining, NY, 1997).

Horse Handling & Grooming, by Cherry Hill (Storey Books, Pownal, VT, 1997). This step-by-step photo guide will help teach you the basics of horse handling and grooming.

Horse Health Care, by Cherry Hill (Storey Books, Pownal, VT, 1997). This is a step-by-step photo guide to basic horse health care.

Horsekeeping on a Small Acreage, by Cherry Hill (Garden Way Publishing, Pownal, VT, 1990). Before you take your horse home, read this.

Horse Owner's Veterinary Handbook, by James M. Giffin, M.D., and Tom Gore, DVM (Howell Book House, New York, NY, 1989). The doctors describe illnesses and ailments affecting horses to help you decide when you need to call the veterinarian and when you don't.

Horse Sense, by John J. Mettler Jr., DVM (Garden Way Publishing, Pownal, VT, 1989). This easy-to-read book is a great primer on basic horse care and laced with fascinating tales by Dr. Mettler.

How to Be Your Own Veterinarian (Sometimes), by Ruth B. James, DVM (Alpine Press, Mills, WY, 1990). This is another book you should have on your shelf if you buy a horse.

How to Build Small Barns & Outbuildings, by Monte Burch (Storey Books, Pownal, VT, 1992).

Lyons on Horses, by John Lyons and Sinclair Browning (Doubleday, New York, NY, 1991). Outstanding way to approach horse training.

101 Arena Exercises, by Cherry Hill (Storey Books, Pownal, VT, 1995). Need direction while you're working in the arena? Provides lots of exercises you can do with your horse, whether you ride English or Western.

Practical Eventing, by Sally O'Connor (Press of Whittet and Shepperson, Richmond, VA, 1980). A good guide and quite understandable, even for the novice.

Taking Up Riding as an Adult, by Diana Delmar (Storey Books, Pownal, VT, 1998). Find out more about how to select a lesson barn, prevent injuries while working around horses and riding, and decide if you're ready for that first horse. There's also an up-to-date health chapter, and lots of ideas for activities with your riding and nonriding friends and family.

Training Hunter Jumpers and Hacks, by Brig. Gen. Harry Chamberlain (D. Van Nostrand Co., Princeton, NJ, 1937). This book is out of print but you can find it if you tool around a little. Excellent section on conformation.

Training the Three Day Event Horse and Rider, by James C. Wofford (Doubleday, New York, NY, 1995). Excellent section on conformation.

Videos

Conformation Evaluation, by Dr. Dewitt Owen (Uniquely Equine, Finchville, KY). Excellent guide to conformation faults and you can see what happens with each fault as the horse moves.

Leading and Loading Safely, by John Lyons (Farnam Video Collection). Shows you the safest way to teach a horse to load and how to teach good ground manners.

Glossary

Aids: Attributes or tools that assist you in riding. Natural aids include your seat, legs, hands, voice, and balance. Artificial aids include reins, spurs, and riding crops.

Back at the knee: A conformation fault seen from the side, in which the knees look bowed toward the rear of the horse. This corresponds to hyperextended knees in people.

Barn sour: A horse that does not care to leave the barn to be ridden. Such horses may be rude or in some cases dangerous, because they may bolt to run back to the barn.

Barrel racing: A timed event in Western riding in which each horse and rider must complete a cloverleaf pattern around three standing barrels.

Bars of the mouth: Horses have teeth for clipping grass in the front of their mouths, and molars for grinding it up in the back. Between the two kinds of teeth is a gap that nicely accommodates a bit. That place is known as the bars, which are the mandibular, or jaw, bones. They're covered by mucous membranes.

Base narrow: As seen from the front, a horse that's wider at the chest than at the feet.

Base wide: As seen from the front, a horse that's wider at the feet than at the chest.

Blocking: Injecting a medication that blocks nerve sensation.

Bute: Short for phenylbutazone, it's a common anti-inflammatory and pain medication for horses.

Cannon bone: The long bone of the front leg that extends from the knee to the ankle. On the hind leg the cannon extends from hock to ankle. Books from England sometimes refer to the hind cannon as the "shannon."

Coggins test: A blood test for equine infectious anemia (EIA) that's required before horses cross state lines, are sold at auction, or come onto the grounds at many shows. Although a local veterinarian draws the blood, the test is always run at a state laboratory. It may take two weeks to get results back, so plan ahead for this test. If a horse fails he may be retested, but if he fails again, the state may require him to be destroyed or permanently quarantined.

Colic: A general term describing pain in the digestive system. Colic corresponds roughly to stomachache in people. It may turn out to be nothing serious, or it may be life threatening.

Combined training/eventing: A sport that encompasses three different disciplines of riding: dressage, cross country, and stadium jumping.

Conformation: The way a horse is conformed, or put together. If all his characteristics are close to the ideal the horse is said to have good conformation, or to be well made.

Contest events: A group of timed classes at Western shows that have in common the element of speed. They include barrel races, pole bending, flag races, and others.

Contest horse: A horse used in contest events. Contest horses need to be fast and agile. Depending on the events the horse is used in he may or may not need to stop well. Some retired contest horses are extremely difficult to stop.

Coronary band: The area of soft tissue immediately above the hoof. This area, also known as the coronet or coronet band, is highly vascular and quite sensitive.

Cow hocks: A conformation fault seen from the rear, in which the hocks appear to point toward each other.

Crest: The part of the horse's neck along which the mane grows.

Cribbing: A stable vice of horses in which the horse locks his front teeth on something solid and, with his mouth open, swallows air. Confirmed cribbers may have difficulty maintaining weight because they'd rather crib than eat. Whether or not cribbing causes colic is controversial. Cribbers may damage stall doors and fencing by their behavior, but the use of a cribbing strap will discourage it.

Cross-country riding: Horse and rider jump a series of natural or natural-looking obstacles that may include creeks, fences, and ditches.

Cross-ties: A method of tying a horse in which each side of his head is fastened to a separate rope that's affixed to a secure post.

Croup: As seen from the side, the part of the horse's topline extending from the hip to the base of the tail.

Cutting: Horse and rider demonstrate their ability to cut, or separate one steer from a herd and prevent the steer from rejoining the herd until the rider chooses to allow it.

Docked: A tail that has been cut off above the end of the tailbone, or dock, is said to have been docked. This procedure leaves a horse unable to swish flies with his tail. Long ago, in Europe, docking was thought to be very stylish on high-stepping carriage horses. It's now only seen on some larger Hackney ponies and Draft Horses.

Dressage: Horses and their riders individually perform a series of prescribed movements and are judged on their skill for each movement.

Encephalomyelitis: Sleeping sickness that horses contract from insects. There's more than one variety of this disease, for which horses should be vaccinated.

Farrier: The professional who shoes horses.

Fescue: A tufted perennial grass that can carry a fungus harmful to pregnant mares.

Float: Sharp edges and points on the horse's teeth are leveled off with a tool called a dental float.

Girth: In English riding, the name of the wide strap that runs behind a horse's front legs to secure a saddle in place. In Western riding it's known as a cinch.

Halter classes: Horse show classes in which the horse is judged only on conformation. The horse is led into the show ring wearing only a halter. At some shows these are also called Strip classes.

Hands: Horses are measured in units called hands. One hand is 4 inches. The horse is measured in a straight line from the ground to the highest point of his withers.

Heritable: A trait that may be passed on through inheritance. Parrot mouth is a heritable trait; a broken tooth is not.

Hocks: The joint above the ankle in the rear leg of a horse.

Hot/Hottest: In terms of horse temperament, *hot* means high strung, fiery, flighty, or nervous. Some Thoroughbred racehorses are considered hot.

Hunter: In the hunter division at horse shows, horses are judged on how perfectly they jump each fence and on their way of going. Form counts.

HYPP (hyperkalemic periodic paralysis): A genetic defect in some Quarter Horses (less often in Appaloosas and Paints) that can be traced back to one sire named Impressive. Carriers may or may not become ill, developing problems such as tremors, seizures, or even sudden collapse and death. If diagnosed, the horse can sometimes be helped with dietary adjustments and medication; sometimes he can't be helped.

Impaction colic: When a horse is unable to pass fecal material or when there's foreign material (such as a plastic bag or bits of rubber fence that he has eaten) lodged in his intestine, he's said to have an impaction.

Influenza: Equine influenza causes symptoms similar to the flu in people. If you often show or take your horse to places where there are other horses, you'll need to vaccinate against the flu about every two months.

Jumper: In the jumper division at horse shows, horses are scored by how many jumping faults they accumulate in a round. Faults are given for knocking down rails and refusing fences. The rounds are also scored for time. Form doesn't much matter.

Laminitis: This disease involves an inflammation of the laminae, which are sensitive tissues in the horse's feet. If it progresses and the laminae break down, a bone in the bottom of the foot known as the coffin bone rotates, and this is called founder.

Longe: A word spelled and pronounced many strange ways. It comes from the French word *longe,* which means "long." It refers to a long line that serves as a training aid: The horse is attached to this line and worked in a large circle around the handler. The most common U.S. spellings are now *lunge* and, less often, *longe.*

Mutton withered: A horse with very low withers.

Navicular bone: A small pyramid-shaped bone in the middle of the foot that serves as a pulley for a tendon. If the navicular bone becomes pitted and rough the tendon does not slide smoothly, and this causes the horse pain.

Offset knees: A conformation fault seen from the front, in which the long bone connecting the shoulder to the knee doesn't line up with the long bone connecting the knee to the ankle. When this fault occurs, the long axis of the knee won't be vertical, but will slant.

Ophthalmoscope: A veterinary device for looking at the internal structures of the eye.

Over at the knee: A conformation fault seen from the side, in which the knees look like they're about to buckle forward.

Parrot mouth: Overbite in a horse. As seen from the side, the upper jaw extends over the lower jaw the way a parrot's upper beak extends over the lower beak.

Pastern: The section of the lower leg that connects the hoof with the ankle.

Pig eyed: A horse with small eyes.

Points: The legs, mane, tail, and tips of the ears. Horses that are bays have black points: black mane, black tail, black lower legs, and black on the ear tips.

Poll: The highest point on the top of the horse's head.

Reining: A popular Western riding event in which each horse and rider works a predetermined pattern.

Rhinopneumonitis: An infectious, flulike disease in horses that may be prevented with vaccination.

Roan: A color in which some individual hairs are two colors: One is the main color of the horse; the other is white. Roaning softens the main color of the horse. If the roan horse is chestnut or sorrel, it is called a red roan. The face and the legs are red, the body a softer, lighter red. A very light red roan, with a flaxen mane, is called a strawberry roan. If the roan horse is dark brown or black, it is called a blue roan. The face and legs are black and the body a soft gray blue.

Roman nose: As seen from the side, the horse's head will have a definite convex profile, like the human aquiline noses admired by the ancient Romans.

Sickle hocks: A conformation fault seen from the side, in which the horse's hocks, and thus his lower hind legs, seem to arc slightly forward under him. The hocks and legs are shaped a little like an antique farmer's sickle.

Stadium jumping: Horse and rider negotiate a course of fences inside a show ring.

Stock-up: If a horse's lower legs swell slightly around the ankles when he stands in his stall for a while although there's no injury, the horse is said to stock-up. Usually such swelling will vanish when he's exercised.

Strangles: An infectious disease that often causes lymph glands between the horse's jaws to swell with infection.

Tack: The equipment used for riding and handling a horse. This includes saddles, bridles, halters, lead ropes, and so on.

Throatlatch: On a bridle, this is the strap that connects the two sides of the crown piece below the horse's jaw. Its function is to keep the bridle from slipping off the horse's head. It's sometimes called a throatlash. On a horse, as seen from the side, this is the area where the back of the lower jaw connects to the throat.

Thrush: A fungal infection of the area around the frog of the foot that has a characteristically foul odor and causes a black, tarry substance. It's more likely to develop if the horse's feet aren't kept clean or if the horse stands in damp or dirty conditions.

Toe in: A conformation fault in which the horse's feet point toward each other. It corresponds to pigeon toes in people.

Toe out: A conformation fault in which the horse's feet point away from each other. It corresponds to splay feet in people.

Tying up: Also called azoturia or exertional rhabdomyelosis, the horse's muscles become hard and may be damaged. The horse may refuse to move, may sweat, and may have a rapid pulse. The condition is likely to occur in horses, especially draft horses, that are rested for several days without a cutback in grain, and then worked; or in horses, like race and event horses, that do fast hard work.

Way of going: The total picture of the horse as he travels, including manners, presence, and natural impulsion.

Western Pleasure: In a Western Pleasure class, riders are asked to walk, jog, and lope in both directions around the arena.

Withers: The highest point on the back of a horse, corresponding to the nape of the neck on people.

Index

Note: Page numbers in *italic* indicate illustrations and photographs; page numbers in **boldface** indicate color photographs.

Breeds with standard gaits, 37–40, 57–66
Bridles, 98, *98*
"Broke to tie," 33, 120, *121*
Bute (phenylbutazone), 25, 147, 157

C

Cannon bone, 157
Choke, 130
Clipping, 105, *106*, 108
Coffin bone rotation, 92, 137–38
Coggins test, 35, 142–43, 157
"Cold blooded," 59
Colic
    and bedding, 81
    causes of, 18, 81, 92, 133
    defined, 130–31, 157
    and feeding, 92, 133, 148, 151
    management of, 132
    and mouth condition, 18
    and rolling, 131, *131*
    and side biting, 131
    signs of, 131, *131*
    veterinary exam for, 132
    and water, 133
    and worming, 133, 144
Color and markings, 10–11
Combined
    driving, 7, 60
    training/eventing, 7, 157
Competitive trail riding, 5, 38, 40
Conformation
    defined, 14–15, 157
    eyes, 16–17, *17*
    feet, 19, 24–25
    head, 15–16, *16*
    legs, front, 19–21, *20–21*
    legs, hind, 19, 21, *21*
    mouth, *17*, 17–18
    pasterns, 22, *22*, 159
    tails, 23–24, *24*
    withers, 18, *18*, 159
Connemaras, **48**, 63
Contest horses, 6–7, 21, 157
Contracts, 31, 94
Coolers, 109, *109*
Cording bow, 130
Coronary band, 111, 157
"Corrected" feet, 19

Costs of upkeep. *See also* Prices of horses
    boarding, 84
    field-boarding, 84–85
    grooming equipment, 105
    tack, 104
    trainers, 13
    upkeep, general, 3
Country Pleasure classes, 67
Cow-hocked legs, 21, *21*, 157
Cresty-necked horses and laminitis, 138, 157–58
Cribbers, 32, 35, 90, 157
Crossbreds, 62–63
Cross-country riding, 7, 157
Cross-tying, 119, 121–22, *122*, 157
Curb bits, 99, *100*
Cutting
    horses, 5–6, 158
    and sickle-hocked legs, 21, 159
    Western saddles, 103, *104*

D

Dehydration, 134
Diarrhea, 134
Disabled riders, 3–4, 39
Disposition of horse, *2*, 2–3, 10, 13
Draft Horses
    and American Warmbloods, 62
    and cow-hocked legs, 21
    and Warmbloods, 59
Dressage
    as a riding activity, 7, *7*, 158
    saddles, 102, *102*
    and Warmbloods, 60–62
Driving
    combined, 7, 60
    for disabled riders, 4, 39
    miniatures, 4, 39
    Morgans, 7, 40
    ponies, 64, 66
    as a sport, 7, *8*
    Standardbreds, 70
Dutch Warmbloods, **47**, 61
Dwarfs, 39

E

"Easy keeper," 92
Encephalomyelitis vaccination, 145, 158
Endurance riding, 5, 38, 71

riding areas, 87, *87*
stalls, 79, *79*
supplies needed, 116
tack room, 86, *86*
turnouts, 88–89
ventilation and light, 80
and veterinarians, 92–93
walls, 82–83
waters and feeders, 78, *83*, 83–84
Homeowner's insurance, 86
Hoof
    care, 144
    testers, 24, 35
Horse associations, 154–55
Horse factors in buying a horse. *See also* Conformation; Costs of upkeep; Prices of horses; Shopping for a horse; *specific breeds;* Veterinarians
    age, 12, 34–35
    attention, need for, 3
    background of, 13, 15
    color and markings, 10–11
    disposition, *2*, 2–3, 10, 13
    gender, 10
    size, 8–9, *9*
    soundness, 24–25
    vices, 31–33
Horse health. *See also* Colic; Veterinarians
    acetylpromazine, 146–47
    bandage bows, 130
    bowed tendons, 129–30, *130*
    choke, 130
    Coggins test, 142–43, 157
    diarrhea, 134
    encephalomyelitis vaccination, 145, 158
    equine infectious anemia (EIA), 35, 142–43, 157
    equine protozoal myelitis (EPM), 134–35
    eye problems, 136
    foot pulse, 139
    founder, 92, 137–38, 140, 150
    heatstroke, 136
    hoof care, 144
    hyperkalemic periodic paralysis (HYPP), 136–37, 158
    influenza vaccination, 146, 158
    injection warning, 147
    laminitis, 92, 137–38, 150, 158
    navicular disease, 139, *139*, 158
    pain medication, 147
    phenylbutazone (bute), 25, 147, 157
    rabies vaccination, 146

records, 134
rhinopneumonitis vaccination, 145, 159
sole abscess, 140
stool check, 144
strangles, 140–41, 159
teeth floating, 143–44, 158
tetanus vaccination, 142, 145
thrush, 141, *141*, 159
tranquilizers, 25, 35, 146–47
tying up, 141, 159
vaccinations, 145–46
worming, 144–45
wound care, 142
xylazine (Rompun), 147
"Hot blooded," 59, 158
Hunters
    and bandages, 110
    as a riding activity, 6–7, 158
    Thoroughbreds as, 59
    Warmbloods as, 60
Hyperkalemic periodic paralysis (HYPP), 136–37, 158

I

Icelandic Horses, 68
Impaction colic, 133, 158
Indoor riding arenas, 73, 86, *87*
Inexperienced riders and horses, 2, 12
Influenza vaccination, 146, 158
Insurance, 86, 93, 115

J

Jumpers
    and offset knees, 21, 158
    ponies as, 63–64, 66
    as a riding activity, 6–7, 158
    Warmbloods as, 61

K

Kimberwicke bits, 100, *100*

L

Lameness
    and EPM, 135
    examination for, 35
    and feet, 19, 24–25
Laminitis
    causes of, 138
    defined, 137, 158
    and feeding, 92, 150
    signs of, 138

Q

Quarter Horses
    breed standard, 25
    described, **56,** 57–58
    feet, potential problems, 19, 58
    head shape, 16, *16*
    and HYPP, 136–37, 158
    for jumping, 6
    and navicular disease, 58, 139, 158
Quarter Pony, 65
Quick-release knots, 120, *120,* 123

R

Rabies vaccination, 146
Racehorses
    and bandages, 110
    and offset knees, 20–21, 158
    Thoroughbreds, 58–59
Rack (gait), 67
Racking Horse, **43,** 69–70
Registration papers, 63
Reining
    as a riding activity, 5–6, 159
    sickle-hocked legs, 21, 159
    tail wringing and, 23
    Western saddles, 103
Rhinopneumonitis vaccination, 145, 159
Rider factors in buying a horse
    arena riding, 4, *4*
    budget available, 3
    combined training/eventing, 7, 157
    driving, 4, 7, *8*
    experience levels, 2
    goals of, 4–8, *4–8*
    knowledge assessment, 2
    physically challenged, 3–4
    show riding, 5–7, *5–8*
    temperament, *2,* 2–3
    time available, 3
    trail riding, 4–5
Riding. *See also* Riding safety
    areas, 86–87, *87*
    and footing, 127
    lessons, 1
    on pavement, 127
    a prospective horse, 28–29
    social aspect of, 73, 75
    in terrain, unknown, 127
    type and stable choice, 76–77
    water crossing, 127

Riding safety. *See also* Safety around horses
    attire, 126, *126*
    coming home, 128
    girth, checking, 127, 158
    and hair, 128
    helmets, 126, *126*
    and jewelry, 128
    and saddles, 103
    shoes, *126,* 126–27
    tack, checking of, 126
    tips, 127
Road founder, 138
"Roarer," 25
Rocky Mountain Horses, 5, **44,** 70
Rolling and colic, 131, *131*
Roman noses, *16,* 159
Rompun (xylazine), 147

S

Saddlebreds. *See* American Saddle Horse (Saddle-breds)
Saddles
    costs of, 104
    English, *102,* 102–3
    fitting, 101
    overview, 101
    pads, 103–4
    synthetic materials, 102, 104
    Western, 103–4, *104*
Saddleseat riding, 6, *6*
Safety around horses
    for approaching, 118
    attire, 126, *126*
    body language, reading, 13, 119
    coming home, 128
    cross-tying, 119, 121–22, *122,* 157
    fire, 78–79, 83
    girth, checking, 127, 158
    for grooming, 119
    and hair, 128
    halters, 96
    helmets, 126, *126*
    holding, 124
    and jewelry, 128
    leading, 119, *119,123,* 123–24
    panic release snaps, 122, *122,* 123
    quick-release knots, 120, *120,* 123
    rear of horses, avoiding, 119
    rules, 117–18
    and saddles, 103

Other Storey Titles You Will Enjoy

The Basics of Western Riding, by Charlene Strickland. A thorough introduction to Western riding. Safe and effective horse-handling procedures and basic riding techniques are covered. 144 pages. Paperback. ISBN 1-58017-030-7.

Becoming an Effective Rider, by Cherry Hill. Teaches riders how to evaluate their own skills, plan a work session, set goals and achieve them, and protect themselves from injury. 192 pages. Paperback. ISBN 0-88266-688-6.

Getting the Most from Riding Lessons, by Mike Smith. Offers valuable information on learning to ride the fun way, understanding school horses, and working with your instructor. 160 pages. Paperback. ISBN 1-58017-082-X.

Horse Care for Kids, by Cherry Hill. The essentials of horse care in a format and tone perfect for passionate teen and pre-teen horse lovers. Beginning with how to match the right animal with the right rider and progressing through feeding, grooming, stabling, health care, safety, and much more. 128 pages. Paperback. ISBN 1-58017-407-8. Hardcover ISBN 1-58017-476-0.

Horse Handling & Grooming: A Step-by-Step Photographic Guide, by Cherry Hill. Includes feeding, haltering, tying, grooming, clipping, bathing, braiding, and blanketing. The wealth of practical advice offered is thorough enough for beginners, yet useful enough for experienced riders improving or expanding their skills. 144 pages. Paperback. ISBN 0-88266-956-7.

Horse Health Care: A Step-by-Step Photographic Guide, by Cherry Hill. Explains bandaging, giving shots, examining teeth, deworming, exercising, and preventive care. 160 pages. Paperback. ISBN 0-88266-955-9.

Horse Sense: A Complete Guide to Horse Selection & Care, by John J. Mettler, Jr., D.V.M. Provides the basics on selecting, housing, fencing, and feeding a horse, including information on immunizations, dental care, and breeding. 160 pages. Paperback. ISBN 0-88266-545-6.

101 Arena Exercises, by Cherry Hill. This unique wire-bound ringside workout book can be hung up or draped over the rail ring for easy reference. English and Western exercises are fully explained, from the basic skills such as the working walk and jog to the "two squares" and "flying change." 224 pages. Paperback. ISBN 0-88266-316-X.

Starting and Running Your Own Horse Business, by Mary Ashby McDonald. This essential guide shows readers how to run a successful business and how to make the most of their investments in horses, facilities, equipment, and time over short- and long-term periods. 160 pages. Paperback. ISBN 0-88266-960-5.

Taking Up Riding as an Adult, by Diana Delmar. Provides a wealth of information, including riding for exercise and fun, selecting a lesson stable and instructor, and when it's time to buy your first horse. 160 pages. Paperback. ISBN 1-58017-081-1.

Teaching Safe Horsemanship: A Guide to English and Western Instruction, by Jan Dawson. Dawson's goal is to provide both English and Western riding instructors with an effective and safe teaching program. Completely revised and updated this book should be required reading for every instructor, stable owner, and guest ranch manager. 160 pages. Paperback. ISBN 1-58017-515-5.

These and other Storey books are available wherever books are sold and directly from Storey Publishing, 210 MASS MoCA Way, North Adams, MA 01247, or by calling 1-800-441-5700. Or visit our Web site at www.storey.com.